With an extensive introduction and notes by ALEXANDER BENNETT
Author of *Japan: The Ultimate Samurai Guide* and translator of *Hagakure: The Secret Wisdom of the Samurai* and *The Complete Musashi: The Book of Five Rings and Other Works*

INAZŌ NITOBE

BUSHIDO

The Samurai Code of Japan

TUTTLE Publishing

Tokyo │ Rutland, Vermont │ Singapore

"Books to Span the East and West"

Tuttle Publishing was founded in 1832 in the small New England town of Rutland, Vermont [USA]. Our core values remain as strong today as they were then—to publish best-in-class books which bring people together one page at a time. In 1948, we established a publishing outpost in Japan—and Tuttle is now a leader in publishing English-language books about the arts, languages and cultures of Asia. The world has become a much smaller place today and Asia's economic and cultural influence has grown. Yet the need for meaningful dialogue and information about this diverse region has never been greater. Over the past seven decades, Tuttle has published thousands of books on subjects ranging from martial arts and paper crafts to language learning and literature—and our talented authors, illustrators, designers and photographers have won many prestigious awards. We welcome you to explore the wealth of information available on Asia at **Asia at** www.tuttlepublishing.com.

Published by Tuttle Publishing, an imprint of Periplus Editions (HK) Ltd.

www.tuttlepublishing.com

Copyright @ 2019 Alexander Bennett
Cover calligraphy © Michiko Imai

Library of Congress Control Number: 2018951468

ISBN 978-4-8053-1489-0

First edition
26 25 24 23
11 10 9 8 7 6   2310VP

Printed in Malaysia

TUTTLE PUBLISHING® is a registered trademark of Tuttle Publishing, a division of Periplus Editions (HK) Ltd.

Distributed by:

North America, Latin America & Europe
Tuttle Publishing
364 Innovation Drive
North Clarendon
VT 05759 9436, USA
Tel: 1(802) 773 8930
Fax: 1(802) 773 6993
info@tuttlepublishing.com
www.tuttlepublishing.com

Asia Pacific
Berkeley Books Pte Ltd
3 Kallang Sector #04-01
Singapore 349278
Tel: (65) 6741 2178
Fax: (65) 6741 2179
inquiries@periplus.com.sg
www.tuttlepublishing.com

Japan
Tuttle Publishing
Yaekari Building, 3rd Floor
5-4-12 Osaki Shinagawa-ku
Tokyo 141 0032 Japan
Tel: 81 (3) 5437 0171
Fax: 81 (3) 5437 0755
sales@tuttle.co.jp
www.tuttle.co.jp

Table of Contents

To my beloved uncle, Tokitoshi Ota,
who taught me to revere the past and
to admire the deeds of the samurai,
I dedicate this little book

Publisher's Foreword

This attractive little book explaining the "soul of Japan" has had a remarkable welcome and response since it was first published in 1905. Today the demand is as great as ever despite the "Westernization" of Japan.

Possibly the chief reason for the demand is that the book answered and continues to answer, for the Japanese as well as the Westerner, the reason why certain ideas and customs prevail in Japan.

Bushido has been variously defined, but it would seem that the definition most generally accepted is that Bushido is the unwritten code of laws governing the lives and conduct of the nobles of Japan, equivalent in many ways to the European chivalry.

The knights and nobles of feudal Japan were the samurai, retainers of the daimyō. Thus, Bushido was the code of conduct of the samurai, the aristocratic warrior class which arose during the wars of the twelfth century between the Taira and Minamoto clans—and came to glorious fruition in the Tokugawa period.

The samurai cultivated the martial virtues, were indifferent to death and pain in their loyalty to their overlords. Samurai were privileged to wear two swords, which were in turn "the soul of the samurai," according to Nitobe.

Bushido presents the cause of Japan in simple but sincere and very readable terms. The author illustrates the points he presents with parallel examples from European history and literature. Finally and foremost, he believes in the law written in the heart. This book was originally published in 1905 by G. P. Putnam's Sons, New York.[1]

NOTE: Nitobe's footnotes from his original edition are enclosed in square brackets. The majority of footnotes are provided by the introducer to this edition, Alexander Bennett.

[1] Nitobe's book was, in fact, first published in 1900 by Leeds & Biddle, a small publishing house in Philadelphia.

Preface to the First Edition

About ten years ago, while spending a few days under the hospitable roof of the distinguished Belgian jurist, the lamented M. de Laveleye,[1] our conversation turned during one of our rambles[2] to the subject of religion. "Do you mean to say," asked the venerable professor, "that you have no religious instruction in your schools?" On my replying in the negative, he suddenly halted in astonishment, and in a voice which I shall not easily forget, he repeated "No religion! How do you impart moral education?" The question stunned me at the time. I could give no ready answer, for the moral precepts I learned in my childhood days were not given in schools; and not until I began to analyze the different elements that formed my notions of right and wrong, did I find that it was Bushido[3] that breathed them into my nostrils.

The direct inception of this little book is due to the frequent queries put by my wife as to the reasons why such and such ideas and customs prevail in Japan.

In my attempts to give satisfactory replies to M. de Laveleye and to my wife, I found that without understanding feudalism and Bushido, the moral ideas of present Japan are a sealed volume.

Taking advantage of enforced idleness on account of long ill-

---

[1] Better known as an economist, Émile Louis Victor de Laveleye (1822–92) was visited by Nitobe in the spring of 1887.

[2] A walk.

[3] [Pronounced Boóshee-doh´. In putting Japanese words and names into English, Hepburn's rule is followed, that the vowels should be used as in European languages, and the consonants as in English.]

ness, I put down in the order now presented to the public some of the answers given in our household conversation. They consist mainly of what I was taught and told in my youthful days, when feudalism was still in force.

Between Lafcadio Hearn[4] and Mrs. Hugh Fraser[5] on one side and Sir Ernest Satow[6] and Professor Chamberlain[7] on the other, it is indeed discouraging to write anything Japanese in English. The only advantage I have over them is that I can assume the attitude of a personal defendant, while these distinguished writers are at best solicitors and attorneys. I have often thought—"Had I their gift of language, I would present the cause of Japan in more eloquent terms!" But one who speaks in a borrowed tongue should be thankful if he can just make himself intelligible.

All through the discourse I have tried to illustrate whatever points I have made with parallel examples from European history

---

[4] Born on the Greek island of Lefkas, Lafcadio Hearn (1850–1904) was a prominent author, translator and educator in Japan. First arriving in 1890, he embarked on a career teaching at several of Japan's most prestigious schools. He later married the daughter of a former samurai and became a Japanese citizen with the name Koizumi Yakumo. His numerous books and essays, which were widely read in the West, were influential in shaping views on Japan.

[5] Mary Crawford Fraser (1851–1922) married the British diplomat Hugh Fraser in 1874 and was thereafter usually referred to as Mrs. Hugh Fraser. She accompanied her husband on his appointments to Peking, Vienna, Rome, Santiago and Tokyo from 1899. It was these experiences that gave her material for her popular memoirs and novels.

[6] Ernest Satow (1843–1929), an English diplomat, linguist and scholar. Working as an interpreter from 1862 to 1882, he later served as Minister Plenipotentiary to Japan (1895–1900) and then in China (1900–06). His memoirs, *A Diplomat in Japan* (1921), offer fascinating insights into Japan's process of modernization.

[7] Basil Hall Chamberlain (1850–1935), a preeminent British expert in Japanese culture and language, first came to Japan in 1873 and taught at the prestigious Imperial Naval School in Tokyo. In 1886, he was appointed as a professor of Japanese at Tokyo University. Interestingly, it was Chamberlain who offered one of the earliest criticisms of Nitobe's work on Bushido in *The Invention of a New Religion* (1912), in which he refutes that Bushido ever existed.

and literature, believing that these will aid in bringing the subject nearer to the comprehension of foreign readers.

Should any of my allusions to religious subjects and to religious workers be thought slighting, I trust my attitude toward Christianity itself will not be questioned. It is with ecclesiastical[8] methods and with the forms which obscure the teachings of Christ, and not with the teachings themselves, that I have little sympathy. I believe in the religion taught by Him and handed down to us in the New Testament, as well as in the law written in the heart.[9] Further, I believe that God hath made a testament which may be called "old" with every people and nation—Gentile or Jew, Christian or Heathen. As to the rest of my theology, I need not impose upon the patience of the public.

In concluding this preface, I wish to express my thanks to my friend Anna C. Hartshorne[10] for many valuable suggestions.

I. N.

---

[8] Ministerial.

[9] Jeremiah 31:33. "But this shall be the covenant that I will make with the house of Israel; After those days, saith the Lord, I will put my law in their inward parts, and write it in their hearts; and will be their God, and they shall be my people."

[10] The American Anna Cope Hartshorne (1860–1957) came to Japan with her missionary father in the 1880s. Becoming a close and lifelong friend of Inazō Nitobe and Mary Elkinton, she assisted him in the writing of this book. Hartsthorne wrote a book of her own called *Japan and Her People* (1902) in two volumes in which Nitobe returned the favor.

Bridging Eons and Oceans

By Alexander Bennett

Born a Samurai

The year is 1867. Excitement pervades the Nitobe household as relatives and other guests gather in the banquet room to celebrate the "Hakama Ceremony" for five-year-old Inanosuke Nitobe. The *hakama*, a loose pair of trousers worn over a *kimono*, was the uniform of the samurai. Boys from warrior families would wear them for the first time upon turning five. It signified initiation into the samurai community of honor and commencement of the roles and responsibilities that came with this status.

In the middle of the room was a *go* board, a traditional form of chess in which black and white stones are used to capture and control open spaces. Standing atop the board with a shiny new short sword at his waist, symbolic of taking his place in the realm, Inanosuke was now officially an adherent of Bushido, the Way of the warrior. The duty that lay before him as a son of the Nitobe clan was more weighty than usual as his father had died earlier in the year. His samurai training commenced immediately, and he was schooled in the martial arts and the Chinese classics from morning to night. According to custom, Inanosuke Nitobe was renamed Inazō Nitobe in 1872 when he was ten years old.[1] However,

---

[1] To avoid confusion, I will refer to him as Inazō (given name) hereafter. Moreover, apart from in the References section, I will write personal names of Japanese individuals mentioned in this introduction according to the Western

three years earlier, in 1869, the new Meiji government had begun to dismantle class distinctions and the samurai were no longer a legitimate social entity. This monumental change was felt keenly by the young Inazō:

> "When I was told to drop [the sword], not only did my loins feel lonely, but I was literally low in spirit. I had been taught to be proud of being a samurai, whose badge the sword was." (*Nitobe Inazō Zenshū*, vol. 15, p. 508)

Inazō was born on September 1, 1862, the eighth child of Jūjirō Nitobe and his wife Seki. Together with two brothers and four sisters, Inazō belonged to a large warrior family of the picturesque but remote Morioka (also known as Nanbu) domain located around modern-day Iwate and Aomori prefectures. Inazō's father Jūjirō and grandfather Tsutō, who traced their lineage back to the fifth son of Emperor Kanmu (737–806), were instrumental in stimulating the local economy through land reclamation. The Morioka domain had endured devastating crop failure seventy-six times over the course of the Edo period (1603–1868). To alleviate the poverty and famine that plagued the countryside, the Nitobe clan constructed irrigation canals from Lake Towada through to Sanbongi. In 1859, the Inaoigawa waterway was completed, leading to a bountiful rice harvest the following year. Inazō was born shortly after and was, in fact, named after this agricultural triumph. Inazō means "to produce rice."

The Nitobe family was highly respected in the region but not averse to defying their superiors if their conscience demanded it. Jūjirō would spend several months of the year in Edo (present-day Tokyo) on business, devising audacious plans to enhance the do-

---

convention of given name first followed by surname, but will mostly refer to them by their surnames.

main's finances. He was wrongfully accused of illicitly selling silk
to French traders to raise money for his development strategies
and placed under house arrest. Although the charges were later
dropped, a blemish of this magnitude on a samurai's honor was
difficult to reverse. Jūjirō ended up "dying of despair" in 1871 at
the age of forty-eight.

This family tragedy notwithstanding, Inazō's childhood was a
time of mounting social and political tension. After 250 years of
relative stability and national isolation, the scent of revolution was
wafting through the country. Following the visit of the American Commodore Matthew Perry in 1853 in his foreboding "Black
Ships," the Tokugawa shogunate eventually bowed to foreign pressure and reluctantly entered various trade treaties with the West,
opening its ports over the next decade. Displeased with the shogunate's weak stance against foreign incursion, an anti-Tokugawa
movement led by young samurai activists from various domains
plotted to overthrow the government. Aligning with key figures at
the hitherto politically impotent court in Kyoto, troops from five
domains seized the Kyoto palace in January 1868. The emperor
ceremoniously read out a document declaring the reinstatement of
imperial rule after seven centuries of warrior dominance, in what
is known as the Meiji Restoration.

Shogunate resistance during the ensuing eighteen-month
Boshin Civil War proved futile. A new government, with the Meiji
emperor as its symbolic head, was established in Edo (Tokyo) and
set forth on what was destined to be a chaotic journey of modernization and engineering of a new national identity. The samurai's
mantle of authority was dismantled in several stages between 1869
and 1872, and their privileges rescinded with the abolition of feudal
class distinctions. Inazō's career as a samurai was thus short-lived,
but traditional warrior mores instilled by his mother from an early
age were to serve him and his country well with Japan's entry onto
the world stage.

Learning English

One of the many catch phrases that gained currency during the Meiji period (1868–1912) *was wakon-yōsai* ("Japanese spirit, Western knowledge"). To successfully create a modern nation state, Japan saw the need to model itself on the West. The *katana* made way for the canon as Japan borrowed and adapted all manner of foreign conventions. Envisaging the future, Inazō's mother encouraged her son to excel in his studies, which included traditional subjects as well as Western military training and English language instruction. Inazō was well-known among locals as a somewhat mischievous youngster. Quick of temper and quite aggressive, his mother's neighborly visits to apologize for his misdemeanors had become a daily affair. Once his energies were redirected to study, he knuckled down and proved to be a gifted student.

Inazō donned Western-style clothes, replaced his wooden sword with a wooden gun, put down his calligraphy brush and picked up a pen. Intrigued by what he called "crab writing" for the way it moved from left to right on the page instead of from top to bottom, Inazō was keen to learn the foreign tongue beyond the rudimentary ABCs being taught to him by the family doctor.

Forced to convert their hereditary samurai stipends into government bonds, Inazō's uncle, Tokitoshi Ōta (Jūjirō's younger brother), like many former warriors, cashed the bonds in to establish a company and try his hand at navigating the treacherous waters of commerce. The thirty-year-old Tokitoshi, who was managing a clothing store in Tokyo, agreed to adopt the nine-year-old Inazō and his older brother Michirō in August 1871. From then until 1889, Inazō took Ōta as his surname.

Prominent intellectuals of the day, such as Yukichi Fukuzawa (1835–1901), advocated proficiency in English as crucial to Japan's future prosperity. This gave rise to an English language boom of sorts among those who had the foresight and wherewithal to learn it. Inazō and Michirō immediately entered an English school near

Tsukiji in Tokyo where they were taught mainly by foreign instructors. The following year, in 1872, the brothers entered the Kyōkan Gijuku, a private school established in Tokyo by the Nanbu family, former lords of the Morioka domain. In 1873, Inazō joined the English department at the acclaimed Tokyo School of Foreign Languages (re-established as the Tokyo English School in 1874). It was there that he met Marion M. Scott, a language instructor whom he later credited with instilling in him a true passion for learning. Under her tutelage, Inazō delved into English poetry and literature and became acquainted with the Bible. By the age of fourteen, he was competent enough to write an essay titled "The Importance of Introducing Christianity into Japan," which Scott sent as an exhibit to the US Centennial Exposition held in Philadelphia in 1876.

Two experiences during his time at the Tokyo English School were to have a huge effect on Inazō's career. The first was a lecture in which he learned of Japan's backwardness in the field of science and the country's serious lack of experts who could teach the subject. Like his peers, he assumed that expertise in jurisprudence was the surest way to become a civil servant in the Meiji government, widely regarded as the mark of "success" at the time and something that educated elites aspired to.

The other important episode was the Meiji emperor's first visit, in 1876, to the northern regions of Japan. The emperor stayed at the Nitobe family's second home in Sanbongi as he inspected the remarkable deeds of Inazō's grandfather and father. So pleased was the emperor with what he saw, that he rewarded the family with a gift of money and entreated Nitobe descendants to continue their fine work in developing the region. Inazō was not present for the imperial visit but received news via a letter from his mother along with two yen (his portion of the gifted money) with which he purchased a beautifully bound Bible for his studies. These two unrelated events made him think about the Nitobe legacy and the part he should play in it from now on. Deciding that his future lay in agriculture, his next step was to move to the northern island of Hokkaido to study at a newly established government school.

Inazō's College Years

The Hokkaido Colonization Office (HCO) was set up in 1869 to administer the northern island of Japan. Hokkaido was a sparsely populated frontier land but was considered strategically significant. Close to Hokkaido is Karafuto (the Japanese name for Sakhalin) and Kuril Island. Japan and Russia have long been embroiled in a dispute over ownership of these territories. In 1876, the HCO opened the Sapporo Agricultural College (SAC, now Hokkaido University) to produce graduates who could promote settlement in the region. This would keep former samurai usefully engaged in farming the land and ready for mobilization should Russia have designs on the territories. With costs covered by the government, entry into the college was competitive, but Inazō and his peers from the Tokyo English School, Kanzō Uchimura and Kingo Miyabe, were successful in their applications.

The foreign expert employed to formulate the curriculum at the new college was William Smith Clark, a professor and co-founder of the Massachusetts Agricultural College in the United States. He was a popular teacher and his motto, "Boys, be ambitious," is still quoted in Japan. Clark taught agriculture, science and English, but his pedagogical style emphasized the liberal arts, physical education and moral studies based on readings from the Bible. Students needed to be sixteen to qualify for entry. Being fifteen when the school opened, Inazō and his friends joined the second intake of students in 1877.

Clark was only at the school for a year before heading back to the United States, so the second group never received instruction from him directly. Nevertheless, his rules and educational policies were to have a lasting effect. For example, he introduced the controversial "Covenant of Believers in Jesus." Sixteen of the first intake of students converted to Christianity and were eager to add fresh faces to their devout circle of youthful Japanese Christians. Inazō already had an interest in Christianity through his English lessons in Tokyo, and he signed the covenant one month after arriving at SAC. The following year, on June 2, 1878, Inazō was formally baptized, along with Uchimura and Miyabe, by Merriman Colbert Harris, the American consul to Hakodate from 1873 and the first Protestant missionary to Hokkaido. Inazō took Paul as his Christian name, Uchimura became Jonathan and Miyabe, Francis. They would congregate after class to debate Christian doctrine with unbridled enthusiasm and became known as the "Sapporo Band."

Most classes at the college were conducted in English. Inazō's friends insisted on calling him "Actiibu" (active) rather than Paul, a nickname they gave him because of his hyperactive nature. Extraordinarily driven in everything he did, Inazō shone in academia as well as sports like the long jump, sumo, and even baseball. As he became increasingly obsessed with matters of faith, his friends coined yet another nickname for him, "Monk." This was not so much a reflection of Inazō's religious zeal as his efforts to come to terms with the Christian doctrine. There were certain things about Christianity that Inazō had difficulty accepting and so he spent countless hours in the library pouring over books about philosophy and religion. Losing himself in books was also a mechanism for dealing with the bouts of depression he was to experience at the college.

During the summer break of his third year, Inazō felt a visit to Morioka was long overdue. He had not seen his mother since leaving for Tokyo almost ten years earlier. As fate would have it, a telegram arrived after he had left Sapporo informing him that his mother was very ill and he should return immediately. Unbeknownst to Inazō, his mother passed away two days before he arrived home and the funeral was already over. A heartbroken Inazō returned to SAC to complete his studies but his friends were alarmed at how despondent he had become.

As a result of his voracious appetite for reading, Inazō's eyesight started to deteriorate and he suffered from terrible migraine headaches. His diary from this period is littered with references to his failing emotional and physical state. It was at this troubling time that he came across some prose by the English writer Thomas Carlyle published in an American periodical, the *Independent*. Inspired by the article, Inazō later managed to obtain a copy of Carlyle's novel of philosophical fiction, *Sartor Resartus* (1836), in which he introduces the "Philosophy of Clothes." The main theme of the novel is that the intellectual practices of humanity's most profound spiritual beliefs have become defunct and new ones must be fashioned to suit the changing times, no matter how elusive this may be.

This struck a chord with Inazō. The idea of worshipping God in a way that that seemed forced within the context of his cultural milieu was precisely what he had difficulty reconciling. Carlyle's ideals were, in a sense, a godsend, opening Inazō's eyes to the idea that there were many paths one could take to ascend the same mountain. Interestingly, Inazō's style of prose appears to be heavily influenced by Carlyle's, and he quotes him regularly in his writings.

Crossing the Seas

Inazō graduated from the Sapporo Agricultural College in 1881, but rather than become a servant of the state, he decided to further his education. After a couple of years fulfilling his obligation to the Hokkaido Colonization Office, Inazō applied for entry into Tokyo Imperial University in 1883. It was in reply to a question about his motivation to study literature and economics during the interview with his prospective professor that he uttered his celebrated words, "I wish to become a bridge over the Pacific."

This time his education was self-funded. On top of the financial strain this entailed, Inazō started to have reservations about the quality of the instruction he was receiving. Masasuke Satō, Inazō's

SAC senior who was studying in the United States at the time, sent him a copy of Henry George's influential book, *Progress and Poverty* (1879). Judging by the indifferent reaction by his professor to the book, Inazō concluded that even the most illustrious institution of higher education in Japan was at least five years behind anything in the West. In one of the many letters he wrote (in English) to his old SAC friend Kingo Miyabe, he vents his frustration. "I am getting disgustful of instructions in the University. I thought I could learn very much in it; but no! There are plenty of good books but not plenty of good teachers...." (*Letters to Dr. Kingo Miyabe*, April 20, 1884) He then goes on to criticize most of his instructors, both Japanese and foreign, who lacked the intellectual rigor Inazō sought. Professor Cox, for example, "is simply an old fashioned true-to-rules-of-syntax grammarian. I don't think very highly of his corrections of our essays...."

Inazō then concluded that it was time to test his mettle in the wider world, and so departed for the United States on his birthday, September 1, 1884. In another letter to Miyabe he writes:

> "I shall leave Tokio for America. I go off unprovided with ample funds. I run a risk: it may be too bold. But thinking that life is at best but a bold attempt at adventure, I decide to go.... Pray for me as oft as thou rememberest me...." (*Letters to Dr. Kingo Miyabe*, August 4, 1884)

After spending some time at Allegheny College in Pennsylvania through an introduction from the wife of Reverend Merriman Colbert Harris who had baptized him in Sapporo, he relocated to Johns Hopkins University in Baltimore where he applied to major in history and political science under Herbert Baxter Adams. Adams graciously employed Inazō as an assistant to help with his finances, and he also took on part-time work in the school's library. A senior at Johns Hopkins whom Inazō much admired was Thomas

Woodrow Wilson, the future president of the United States. Wilson was behind the establishment of the League of Nations (forerunner to the United Nations) thirty years later where Inazō was to serve with great distinction as the Under-Secretary-General.

Inazō was stimulated intellectually at Johns Hopkins although he found himself listening more than participating in the discussions that took place. Outside school, he also fell upon another way of making ends meet by lecturing on things Japanese. Inazō was, of course, hardly known to the audience but such was the growing interest in Japan that his talks were well received. "Japonisme," for example, a type of artistic exoticism centered on Japanese cultural motifs, had become a popular trend in the arts worldwide. People were curious about this mysterious country in the Orient, but there were few who could talk about it with authority. Inazō found a niche and became an adept public speaker admired for his excellent communication skills and joviality.

On his way back from classes one day he saw a group of women dressed in "old-fashioned attire." The person he was walking with informed him that they were Quakers. Inazō knew of the Quakers as Carlyle was an admirer of George Fox, the founder of the Society of Friends. Inazō decided to go to one of their Sunday gatherings and what he encountered in their place of worship was a sense of ease that, at last, felt right to him. The building was plain, the people were dressed simply and there was no pastor, organ music or singing of hymns. About 300 people were sitting on wooden benches in quiet prayer experientially accessing "the small light within." He became a member of the Philadelphian Society of Friends in December 1885. Much later, in 1926, Inazō gave a lecture in Geneva in which he stated that Quakerism allowed him to "reconcile Christianity with Oriental thought."

He and Kanzō Uchimura, who was also in the United States at the time, were invited one day to Philadelphia by the Women's Foreign Missionary Association of Friends. They asked the two men about the prospect of establishing a Quaker mission in Japan. Drawing comparison with the indigenous religion of Shinto, both Inazō and Uchimura agreed that the Japanese would relate easily to Quakerism. The Quakers subsequently established the Friends School for Girls in Tokyo in 1887. The school still exists as the Friends Girls Junior and Senior High School, and Inazō maintained a close relationship with this school after returning to Japan several years later.

At a tea party following a Quaker meeting in Baltimore, Inazō became acquainted with a young woman who demonstrated a keen interest in Japan. Mary Elkinton was the daughter of a prominent Philadelphian Quaker family and Inazō found himself smitten by her beauty and intellect. His family had earlier chosen a wife for him in an attempt to dissuade him from going to America, but he was not interested in the slightest, admitting in a letter to Miyabe that he would rather be "entirely free from matri-embarrassment." (October 5, 1884) He had second thoughts after meeting Mary.

After graduating from Johns Hopkins University, Masasuke Satō had returned to Japan in the summer of 1886 to take up a professorial position at his alma mater, the Sapporo Agricultural College. He recommended to the governor of Hokkaido, Michitoshi Iwamura, that Inazō also be given a teaching post at the school. Iwamura agreed, but it was decided that Inazō should first spend several years in Germany on a full scholarship to gain more research experience. This was a golden career opportunity for Inazō. Completing his three years of study at Johns Hopkins in May 1887, he was awarded a Bachelor of Arts degree with his thesis titled "The Intercourse between the United States and Japan." This work was published in 1891.

In 1887, Inazō entered Bonn University, then Berlin University the following year to research agricultural economics and statistics. He went on to study in the Agriculture Department of Halle University in 1889 (the year that he changed his name back to Nitobe from Ōta), receiving his doctorate in 1890 with a thesis written in German about patterns of Japanese land usage. Although his workload was colossal, Inazō always found time to correspond with Mary. They decided to marry after he had completed his studies, a proposal that both Inazō's uncle and Mary's father were initially opposed to. Nevertheless, they were determined to be together with or without the blessing of their families. Inazō returned to Philadelphia on his way back to Japan, and he and Mary were married on New Year's Day, 1891. The ceremony was reported in the *Philadelphia Inquirer* as a noteworthy social event.

Of the many great scholars Inazō became acquainted with during his time in Europe, the esteemed Emile Louis Victor de Laveleye, whom he met in Liege, Belgium, is particularly relevant to this book. Introducing himself in a letter to Laveleye, Inazō was subsequently invited to stay in his family home. The topic of religious education came up one day. Inazō informed the professor that Japanese schools did not promote the teaching of Buddhism or Shinto to pupils. Somewhat dumbfounded, the professor replied, "How, then, do you teach children morality?" Inazō did not have an immediate answer. This was to come several years later with the publication of Bushido in 1900.

A Career of Ebbs and Flows

Inazō's remarkable career can loosely be split into three distinct periods. Upon returning from Germany he first became an instructor at the Sapporo Agricultural College, as promised, where he worked for several years. The next important period was when he served as the principal of the First Higher School in Tokyo. The third was his tenure as Under-Secretary-General for the League of Nations in Geneva.

Starting in 1891 as a professor at SAC, Inazō concentrated his energies on publishing research and enhancing the institution's reputation. He also busied himself with translations of a large body of Western literature, such as the work of William Penn. He taught at

other schools as an adjunct professor and opened a Bible school in
the family home, which was frequented by SAC students and others attracted to Christianity. A little-known fact is that Inazō also
introduced the sport of ice hockey to Hokkaido around this time.
In January 1892, the Nitobes were overjoyed with the birth of
their first child, a boy they named Thomas. Although I can find no
reference to confirm this, I suspect that Thomas Carlyle may have
been his namesake. Thomas died around a week later, a tragedy
that left them both grief-stricken for some time. (Mary never conceived after this, but they adopted two of Inazō's distant relatives.)
It was Carlyle's writings and the Bible that brought solace to Inazō.
Carlyle's "Mission of Sorrow" ultimately helped him overcome his
grief. He understood that from great tragedy must come inspiration to do good, and that despair is, in fact, necessary for personal
growth. As he observed later:

> "Sincerity of action is the gospel Carlyle preached by
> word and life. For—remember, words are acts and the
> pen in the hand of the good and the great cleaves sharp-
> er than a two-edged sword. The worth of any action is
> estimated by the motive which lies behind it, by the sin-
> cerity which animates it. Hence, in every act, howsoever
> trivial or momentous, we see an idea put to work; we
> see an ideal in the process of realization; we see a spirit
> laboring." (*Thoughts and Essays*, p. 31)

Inazō took a period of leave from SAC and accompanied Mary
to Philadelphia to recuperate. Mary returned to Japan in 1893 with
a considerable donation of $2,000 from the Elkinton family. True to
Carlyle's words, with the money the Nitobes founded a night school
for working-class people and for children who were too poor to receive a formal education. The school, called Enyū Yagakkō (Friends
from Afar Night School), was inaugurated in January 1894 with

Inazō as its principal. Apart from the obvious allusion to Quaker-ism and the financial donations received from friends in the United States, the name of the school in Japanese incorporated the first ideogram of Thomas's name.

Inazō continued to follow a demanding work schedule that started to take its toll on his health. Erwin Baelz, a German phy-sician resident in Japan, diagnosed Inazō as suffering from a "breakdown," which he advised would require several years of convalescence. Following Baelz's advice, Inazō retired from SAC in 1897 and traveled with Mary to Monterey in California to regain his strength in a warmer climate. With no teaching or administra-tive responsibilities to occupy him, Inazō was able to objectively contemplate the significance of Japan and his life experiences.

With Mary's help, Inazō organized his thoughts in *Bushido: The Soul of Japan*, published in 1900. Although a slim volume, and only one of many works by Inazō in English, it was destined to become his most widely known publication. As an introduction to the psyche and culture of the Japanese, it unexpectedly became crucial in Inazō's stated goal of bridging civilizations. I will outline the implications of this book below.

Fully recovered in body and mind, the second stage of Inazō's career began in 1901 when he became an administrator in the Taiwan Government House until 1903. His specialization in ag-riculture paid dividends as he was able to reinvigorate the sugar industry in Taiwan, increasing the yield six-fold in just over a year and making it the fourth largest sugar exporter in the world. His success in bringing the Taiwanese economy into the black led to his appointment as a professor in the Faculty of Law at the Kyoto Imperial University from 1903 to 1906.

Present-day critics of Inazō's legacy point to his role in Japan's expansionist policies. Japanese intentions for Taiwan were to trans-form the territory into a "model colony," and Inazō's contribution to the economy cannot be overstated here.

Compared to his contemporaries, Inazō championed more humanitarian ideals, beseeching colonial administrators to raise living standards, not simply commandeer resources for the benefit of the "mother country." Korea was declared a Japanese protectorate in 1905 with the signing of the Japan-Korea Treaty, and officially annexed in 1910. As early as October 1905, Inazō had commented on the kind of colonial superiority that Japan should never adopt:

> "If Korea should lose her political independence, her people should at least be paid for it by better treatment from their new masters; but if instead they receive kicks and blows, it is indeed sad proof that we are unworthy of the name and place of an expanding nation. If our influence in China should foster a 'yellow peril' in its worst forms, to the menace of civilization and to the detriment of humanity, it will only argue that we have no right to hegemony over Asia." (*Thoughts and Essays*, p. 145)

Of course, many would argue that Japan never had the right to hegemony over Asia and that such a declaration reeked of paternalistic arrogance. But ethnocentrism was a prevalent feature of any colonial regime at the time. Apart from the obvious economic benefits, as well as the perceived need to appropriate territory to accommodate a rapidly growing domestic population, Japan saw itself as the only power in Asia with the means to bring about political stability in a sphere of Asian "co-prosperity." As it happened, the Japanese colonizers earned a bad reputation among indigenous populations for being unsympathetic taskmasters. Inazō was an ardent opponent of the "kicks and blows" that people in protectorates were inevitably subjected to. However, contradictions arising from the clash between his sense of national pragmatism and his international idealism cannot be easily reconciled. His guarded reaction to the Manchurian Incident in 1931, for example, fueled Inazō's detractors and baffled his supporters, but more on this below.

The second important stage in Inazō's career was his appointment, in 1906, as principal of the prestigious First Higher School
in Tokyo. This was essentially a preparatory school for the Tokyo
Imperial University and is now the College of Arts and Sciences
at the University of Tokyo. Many of the students who attended the
school were destined to become the country's top administrators
(even now), and the opportunity to instill his own "gentlemanly"
brand of liberal education aimed at acquiring "outer gentleness and
inner fortitude" was one that he relished.

His tenure lasted until 1913. On the whole, Inazō was admired
by the staff and students but his methods were often controversial.
Some hardliners were aggrieved by Inazō's leaning as a "tattler of
pacifism," which would transform boys into effete weaklings "be-
reft of manly spirit." While carrying out his responsibilities at the
First Higher School, he continued writing, lecturing, establishing
and advising new schools, particularly those related to the education of women. He was also simultaneously employed, in 1909, as
a professor of colonial policy in the Faculty of Law at Tokyo Imperial University.

Although Inazō was trained as a scholar and was equipped
with qualifications from some of the world's most highly esteemed
universities, much of his writing from this period was crafted for
popular magazines or periodicals that published articles on morality. As such, Inazō was not immune to scathing critiques from
academics or those who found issue with his unconventional at-
titudes, but this rarely bothered him. True to his calling as an educator, he found validation in touching the hearts of the common
people and guiding young men and women in their development.
He also became a prominent spokesman for women's affairs and
gained a wide following with his numerous articles in the dominant women's magazines, *Fujin Gahō* and *Fujin Sekai*. He was not a
political feminist as such but championed the role of women in the

workplace and was strident in his opposition to the constraints imposed by a popular adage of the day, "Good Wives, Wise Mothers."

Inazō was selected to tour the United States in 1911 as the first exchange professor on the Carnegie Endowment for International Peace program. He was especially irked by American policies toward Japanese immigrants at the time, and an article he wrote in August 1904 reveals how sensitive he was to bigotry aimed at Japan:

> "Does Europe really believe that her civilization is a rickety framework to be easily upset by a horde of Asiatics? Go to! It is nonsense this, the whole gabbling and babbling about 'The Yellow Peril.'" (*Thoughts and Essays*, p. 75)

He delivered 166 speeches to an estimated 40,000 people at many of America's finest universities, including his alma mater, Johns Hopkins. His purpose was to try and foster greater understanding between Japan and the United Sates. These lectures were collated and published as *The Japanese Nation: Its Land, Its People, and Its Life* (1912). His speeches and writings to foreign audiences were typically crafted to facilitate an appreciation of Japan's cultural idiosyncrasies. With Japanese audiences, however, he would go to great lengths to extol Western wisdom in order to accelerate social and technological progress. He thus adopted the dual role of "defender of Japan" and "challenger of Japan," depending on his intended audience. In an essay he wrote in 1904, for example, he chided his countrymen for their tendency to equate Japanese "uniqueness" with the notion of "island country spirit" (*shimaguni konjo*), a generalization that is often heard to this day:

> "How often do we hear the disparaging term Shimaguni konjo, insular spirit, applied to the mental limitations and moral aberrations of our own selves! The expres-

sion has become a hackneyed explanation of our lack of sympathy, the restrictions of our intellectual horizon, the smallness of our world-conception. Not only has it become an explanation of, but a stereotyped excuse for, our racial defects. This implies two unfortunate ideas. One is that we make our defects a natural and therefore unavoidable consequence of our geographical location. The other is that we make ourselves—I mean individuals, each one of us—largely irresponsible for our frailties." (*Thoughts and Essays*, p. 52)

He presented a series of important lectures titled "The Foundation of the American Nation" at Tokyo Imperial University in 1918 as part of the inauguration of the Hepburn Chair of American History and Government. Gifted by Barton A. Hepburn, a wealthy New York banker and philanthropist, the event has been referred to as representing the beginning of American studies in Japan. In the same year, he became the first president of Tokyo Women's Christian College.

Inazō's life took on unprecedented international importance when he was appointed Under-Secretary-General of the League of Nations in 1920, the third important period of his career. This distinguished position took him to the League's headquarters in Geneva for seven years, where his affable nature and skill in the art of diplomacy earned him the moniker "Star of Geneva." Nine times out of ten he was chosen to address audiences on behalf of the League in place of his superior, Secretary-General Eric James Drummond, who was not a confident or willing public speaker. Drummond himself said of Inazō, "He gives his audiences a deep and lasting impression."

Inazō was responsible for directing the International Bureau and served as a founding member of the International Committee for Intellectual Cooperation (ICIC, later to become UNESCO). Ever the avid linguist, he attended the World Congress of Esperanto in Prague in 1921 as the League's representative and recommended that Esperanto be adopted as the working language. Although many accepted his proposal, it was eventually vetoed by the French delegate.

Another well-known episode during Inazō's tenure was his work in settling a territorial dispute over the Åland Islands between Sweden and Finland. An agreement was reached through some deft political negotiations by Inazō and his determination to find a peaceful resolution. The islands would remain under Finnish control but be granted autonomy and disarmed. This successfully staved off conflict in the region and is remembered as the Nitobe Settlement. The settlement became a prototype for non-violent arbitration of minor international conflicts in the modern era. Inazō resigned from the post in 1926 but was retained as a committee member of the ICIC.

Returning from Geneva, he became a member of the House of Peers in the Japanese Diet. By now a household name in Japan, his services were in high demand. He accepted a position on the editorial board of the English-language *Osaka Mainichi* newspaper in which he wrote a popular column on a range of issues. Among the many posts he accepted was as advisor to the union movement and the Morioka Farmer's Co-operative.

Had he retired from international politics following his term at the League of Nations, he would have avoided the dark storm clouds forming on the horizon. Being the "go to man" for things Japanese at a time when Japan was starting to flex its military muscle, Inazō found himself in an unenviable position, open to hostility from all quarters.

Inazō's involvement with the Institute of Pacific Relations (IPR) was to be his final mission to promote international understanding. The IPR was an international NGO formed in 1925 to provide a forum for examining various issues arising between Pacific Rim nations. Inazō was nominated in 1929 by Junnosuke Inoue (1869–

1932) to take over his position as IPR Japan Council Chairman. Inoue was assassinated in 1932 by a member of the ultranationalist terrorist group Ketsumeidan when serving as Minister of Finance. Japan had become a dangerous place to voice political opinion, especially if it ran counter to the rising militaristic rhetoric.

Inazō's annoyance at prejudicial immigration policies in the United States motivated him to accept the position. Up until the 1924 Immigration Act, 146 Japanese were admitted annually into the United States as immigrants through the so-called Gentleman's Agreement of 1907. With this Act, Japan was deprived of any change in the quota for immigration. Inazō was clearly positioned in title, experience and personal network to encourage a reconsideration of the Act. Together with Eiichi Shibusawa (1840–1931), a distinguished business leader and the head of a committee on Japanese-American relations, Inazō strove to mitigate distrust forming between the two countries. The efforts of the two men appeared to be on the verge of paying off when the Manchurian Incident broke out in September 1931.

The Manchurian Incident represented a rise in extreme nationalistic strategies in Japan with regard to overseas expansion. Japan retained special rights in Manchuria throughout the first three decades of the twentieth century. Believing that neutrality of the region was vital for the defense of Korea, the growing nationalism and political instability in China under Chiang Kai-Shek, and the ever-present threat of Russian infiltration into their territories, compelled Japan's field army in Manchuria to "protect" Japanese interests in the region. The London Naval Treaty of 1930, which forced Japan into an inferior 5:5:3 battleship ratio with the United States and United Kingdom, followed by worldwide condemnation for its actions in Manchuria, resulted in Japan's withdrawal from the League of Nations on March 27, 1933.

Anti-Japanese sentiment was gaining momentum, and Inazō, the "defender of Japan," was doing his utmost to present his coun-

try's case. Inazō, the internationalist "challenger of Japan," also had
to contend with his countrymen. A notorious domestic incident
known as the Matsumoto Affair had an irrevocable effect on his
reputation. During a lecture tour in the southern regions of Japan,
Inazō, in casual conversation with acquaintances observed that Japan was in danger of being destroyed by either "militarists or com-
munists." He also condemned the government's explanation for its
recent military action in Shanghai (1932). A reporter, supposedly
unaware that the comments were meant to be off the record, published Inazō's observations in the *Kainan* newspaper (a rival to the
Osaka Mainichi).

The repercussions were swift and far-reaching. Despite being
hospitalized for arthritis, Inazō was summoned to explain his comments in front of the Imperial Reservists Association (Imperial
Veterans Association), a politically active group of conservatives
who endorsed militaristic ideology. Under the threat of violence
and accompanied by his bodyguard (his grand-nephew), he tried to
explain how his words were taken out of context but was ordered to
make a public act of contrition on the spot. He yielded and bowed
his head in apology. This action, in turn, was construed by former
colleagues in the League of Nations and the United States as com-
promising his beliefs in defense of the rise of militarism.

Caught between a rock and a hard place, Inazō's reputation was
inextricably linked to international perceptions of Japanese government actions. The fact that he had written his bestselling book
extolling the ethos of the Japanese warrior three decades earlier did
not help his estimation among Westerners with the burgeoning of
Japanese hawkishness. But, as he confessed in his editorial jottings
for the *Osaka Mainichi* on May 16, 1933:

> "A good internationalist must be a good nationalist
> and vice versa. The very terms connote it. A man who
> is not faithful to his own country cannot be depended

on for faithfulness to a world principle. One can serve
best the cause of internationalism by serving his country. On the other hand, a nationalist can best advance
the interests and honor of his country by being internationally minded."

Against the advice of his family and friends, Inazō embarked
on another tour of the United States with Mary in April 1932. Although he had previously vowed never to set foot in America until
the Immigration Act was amended, he felt duty bound to explain
the historical and economic circumstances underlying Japan's actions in Manchuria. To this end, he gained access to dignitaries
such as President Hoover, and delivered more than a hundred lectures over ten months. His talks were popular, but it is doubtful
whether his Manchurian message was accepted, especially with his
nuances of American hypocrisy and double standards in matters
of protecting national interests. His speeches at the University of
California, where he was a visiting professor, were published posthumously as *Lectures on Japan* (1936).

Inazō was to make one last trip to North America in 1933 to
participate in the Institute of Pacific Relations conference in the
Canadian city of Banff. Inazō had chaired the third such conference
held in Kyoto in 1929. In his address to the delegates he implored,
"Is it too much to hope then that in the intimate contact of nation-
als from all over the Earth, the day will gradually come when not
passion but reason, when not self-interest but justice will become
the arbiter of races and nations?"

After the Banff conference, Inazō went to Victoria where he
joined Mary who was recovering from a mild heart attack. It was
their intention to travel around the United States, but Inazō himself succumbed to a serious illness from which he would not re-
cover. He passed away unexpectedly on October 15, 1933, at the
age of seventy-two. The cause of death was pancreatitis. A service

7

was held at the Wesley United Church in Vancouver. Mary took his ashes back to Japan and another memorial service was held in Tokyo, which over 3,000 people attended.

Inazō's name and achievements, however, were soon forgotten when the world became engulfed in a maelstrom of chaos for fifteen long years. The Asian time bomb exploded with the Second Sino-Japanese War in 1937. What followed was unbridled Japanese military and economic expansionism throughout Asia and the Pacific. In 1940, Japan became the third Axis wheel in the Tripartite Pact with Nazi Germany and Italy. In 1941, the imperial forces set about "liberating" Indo-China from the French and Indonesia from the Dutch, and invaded the British colonies of Hong Kong, Burma, North Borneo, Malaya, Singapore, the Philippines and various Pacific islands. And, of course, there was the audacious bombing of Pearl Harbor in December 1941.

The empire's soldiers were expected to sacrifice their lives for the emperor and state, just as samurai had done as loyal retainers in years gone by. The education system focused on preparing youth for the demands of war and Inazō's *Bushido: The Soul of Japan* was selected as a textbook for the ultra-nationalistic moral education curriculum. In the aftermath of World War II, Bushido was renounced as a noxious component of ultra-nationalism and deemed unsuitable for a postwar democratic society. Even martial arts like judo and kendo were banned in schools and in the community because of the dangerous martial spirit they exemplified.

Things began to change in the 1960s and 1970s when Japan's economic miracle took place. By the 1980s, interest in Bushido was rekindled and admired as being the "source" of the latent energy that enabled Japan to rise from the ashes and thrive on the international stage. A popular genre of literature called *Nihonjin-ron* (theories of [the uniqueness of] Japanese people), which sought to illuminate Japan's unique traits leading to such prosperity, became fashionable in Japan and abroad. Suddenly, Inazō seemed more relevant than ever before, to the extent that his portrait graced the 5,000-yen note from 1984 until 2005. Inazō Nitobe the man, his book *Bushido: The Soul of Japan*, and his global accomplishments and vision for Japan were celebrated as far-sighted and thoroughly deserving of adulation. There is now a plethora of modern Japanese translations of *Bushido* lining the shelves of bookstores, big and small, throughout Japan. His interpretation of Bushido is arguably the most influential source for contemporary Japanese understanding of samurai ethics. But what exactly is Bushido?

The Meaning of Bushido

Literally the "Way of the warrior," the term Bushido first emerged around the beginning of the Edo period (1603–1868) but did not come into popular use until class distinctions were abolished following the Meiji Restoration of 1868. Many other terms have been used throughout Japan's history to denote the ideals and lifestyle of professional men-at-arms, for example, *kyūba-no-michi* (Way of the bow and horse), *budō* (martial Way), *otoko-no-michi* (manly Way) and *shidō* (Way of the gentry). There were many more that most modern Japanese people have never heard of or used.

It was not until the mid to late Meiji period (1868–1912) that the word Bushido came into vogue to represent all that was noble in the Japanese people through a shared cultural and ideological connection between modern Japanese and the samurai of olden times. True samurai, the elite of society, would have been outraged by the notion of commoners claiming to personify their values or way of life. In the twentieth century, however, Bushido became an all-encompassing term for the culture, principles and lifestyle of samurai from all time periods. It was seen as representing the intrinsic morality or spirit of the Japanese people.

In the context of Japanese history, the samurai rose to prominence at the end of the twelfth century with the establishment of the Kamakura shogunate by Minamoto-no-Yoritomo (1147–99).

Special bonds of loyalty formed between the medieval lords and their retainers centered on the reciprocal relationship of "service for favor." Absolute loyalty formed the core of the lord–retainer relationship, but underneath this cloak of fealty lay pragmatic considerations. The onus was very much on the overlord to keep his men content. Loyalty was a contractual arrangement that could be, and often was, renounced depending on the circumstances.

The fragility of this bond was evident in the period of the Warring States (1467–1568) when unquestioned allegiance to one's overlord was often conveniently forsaken for personal gain. Alliances and promises were broken as quickly as they were made. It was a volatile period in which the rise or demise of a great *daimyō* warlord, his *ie* (house) and his clan were only a treacherous back stab away. Vassals were known to turn the tables on their superiors in acts of treachery known as *gekokujō* (lower overturning upper). The uncertainty of life led to the proliferation of "house rules" (*kakun*), laws (*hatto*) and prescripts outlining model samurai behavior, a clear indication that model behavior was not always the norm. Early codification of idioms of honor and exemplary conduct provided guidelines for survival of the clan.

Following the establishment of the Tokugawa shogunate in 1603, the reality of war slowly but surely became a thing of the past. The Shimabara Rebellion of 1637 was the last major armed conflict, and as social stability prevailed from then on, samurai faced an identity crisis. Their distinctive sense of honor was based on acts of violence and valor in the fray, but opportunities to demonstrate their prowess were few and far between. The warrior spirit needed to be redefined.

Medieval honor-centric virtues of loyalty and sacrifice continued but were juxtaposed with Confucian principles of universal order, lawfulness and cultural refinement. Samurai were transformed from men-of-war into salaried bureaucrats gathered in castle towns and tasked with administering their domain's government. The shogunate introduced several policies, such as National Seclusion (*sakoku*) and the alternate-year attendance system (*sankin kōtai*) in the capital of Edo to prevent any troublemaking or the secret accumulation of wealth and military strength among the provincial ruling elite away from the watchful eye of the government. The samurai were tamed.

While conflict was still fresh in the samurai's collective memory, warrior literature began to position the art of war in a time of peace. Arguably, *Gorin-no-sho* (1645) by Japan's most celebrated swordsman, Musashi Miyamoto, is a fine example. His magnum opus explains the principles of battle as the "Way of Combat Strategy." He demonstrates how these principles are applicable to all aspects of life. In fact, Musashi entreats that daily conduct and attention to detail in peacetime should be no different than in times of war.

With the passing of time, such views came to represent a romantic ideal rather than the reality of samurai life. The focus of honor shifted from violence to obedience. Neo-Confucian scholars such as Sokō Yamaga (1622–85) proposed new justifications for the existence of professional warriors in a time of peace. Because warriors no longer fought in pitched battles or contributed to the production of food or goods, Sokō concluded that they should instead dedicate themselves to the service of their lord and domain (= the people) while continuing to develop their mental and physical preparedness to act should the need arise. Samurai, he argued, were duty bound to serve as perfect moral examples dedicated to duty and to upholding the peace.

Sokō's student, Yūzan Daidōji (1639–1730), author of a popular book among urbanized samurai called *Budō Shoshinshū* (c. 1725), encouraged samurai to persevere with their calling and lifestyle for as long as they could to serve their lords. He urged samurai to always be mindful of the potential for violence and to avoid getting into fights. Should a samurai squander his life exchanging blows in some frivolous affair of honor, he would bring shame upon him-

self and his lord. Instead, he argued, a samurai should focus on the
weighty obligation of service and correct conduct in every aspect
of his life.

Yūzan's contemporary, Jōchō (Tsunetomo) Yamamoto (1659–
1719), also admonished apathetic younger generations of samurai to be aware of death, but for different reasons. Famous for the
phrase "The Way of the warrior is found in dying," his *Hagakure*
(1716) is often interpreted as a radical approach that pushes for a
more nihilistic model of behavior. Jōchō was, in fact, reminding
samurai who had lost sight of the duties of their profession to conduct even mundane tasks as if their lives depended on it.

In all cases, honor was gained and sustained through steadfastness in service, wholesomeness in thought and wholeheartedness
in action. This is what qualified samurai to be the political, moral
and intellectual leaders of Edo-period Japan. But it was the samurai's devotion to service that was responsible for their eventual ter-
mination. An exclusive, privileged minority comprising a mere five
percent of the population, it was samurai who instigated the Meiji
Restoration (1868), which replaced their military government with
an imperial one.

Class distinctions were dismantled, but former samurai remained at the vanguard of Japan's modernization and aspects of
their heritage were retained or reinvented in the creation of a new
national identity. This monumental task was accomplished through
various means, such as the media, education and the promulgation
of civil codes. Newly fashioned notions of Bushido that borrowed
components from shared remembrance of a heroic warrior past
were propagated vigorously. Traditional qualities of the samurai,
such as loyalty and self-sacrifice, were promoted as ubiquitous
traits of the Japanese spirit.

Basil Hall Chamberlain (1850–1936), the renowned English
Japanologist, made the following cynical but astute observations
about the burgeoning Japanese nationalism and the "religion of

loyalty" in the later Meiji period:

> "[P]re-existing ideas have been sifted, altered, freshly compounded, turned to new uses, and have found a new center of gravity. Not only is it new, it is not yet completed; it is still in the process of being consciously or semi-consciously put together by the official class, in order to serve the interests of that class, and, incidentally, the interests of the nation at large." (*The Invention of a New Religion*, 1912)

National pride in Japan's samurai past became especially noticeable around the period of the First Sino-Japanese War (1894–95). Success in the Russo-Japanese war of 1904–05 was even more instrumental in recognizing Bushido in Japan and around the world as the core of an intrinsic and admirable strength embodied by the Japanese people. There were even movements in Britain and other countries that sought to emulate this code of honor. For example, the Fabian Society, a predominantly socialist organization founded in 1884, looked to the spirit of Bushido as the reason for Japan's rapid modernization. They saw Bushido as being behind a sense of national duty in all its citizens from bottom to top, and believed it held vital clues for the revitalization of Britain. A prominent member of the Fabian Society, H. G. Wells, wrote *A Modern Utopia* in 1905. This curious book tells the story of two travelers who are transported to a utopian society in a parallel universe ruled by a group of benevolent and wise people known as the "Samurai."

Charles à Court Repington, a former Lieutenant-Colonel in the British Army, who worked as the military correspondent for *The Times*, wrote many articles in praise of this immutable Japanese spirit:

> "We recognize, almost grudgingly and in spite of our-

selves, the existence of a moral force that appears able to
govern and sway the whole conduct of a whole people,
inspiring not a caste, but a nation from highest to lowest
to deeds that are worthy to rank with the most famous
of history or of legend. We want to know what this force
is, whence it comes; the sense of its existence makes us
jealous, uncomfortable, almost annoyed." (*The Times*,
October 4, 1904)

In reaction to the popularity of Inazō's bestseller and the cult
status that ideals of Bushido was gaining in Britain, the Anglican
Church commissioned John Toshimichi Imai (1863–1919), a Japanese Anglican priest working for the South Tokyo diocese, to write
another book on the subject in English. He penned his short book,
Bushido: In the Past and in the Present (1906), first as a series of articles for the popular journal *The East and the West*. His reasons for
writing about Bushido were simple: to downplay the hype. As far
as style and content are concerned, Imai's work is considerably less
effusive than Inazō's. He does not overtly refute what Inazō wrote,
and even picks up on some of Inazō's themes and offers more detail. He concludes that Bushido undoubtedly played an important
role in the shaping of the Japanese nation, but that Christianity
was needed as well to supplement traditional morality in Japanese
people, a conclusion not so different from Inazō's ideals.

At first seen as a favorable force for social change, the positive
international image of Bushido would become negative when the
West's love affair with Japan subsided in the aftermath of World
War I. The martial elements of Bushido were highlighted in the
militaristic 1930s. Tales of gallant warriors like Musashi and early
modern treatises of Bushido, such as *Hagakure*, were perfect propaganda tools for inculcating nationalistic fervor and a samurai-esque
resolve to sacrifice oneself for emperor and state.

Defeat in 1945 meant that Bushido and its trappings fell out of favor. It was perceived as representing a dark, tragic past orchestrated by malevolent militarists that was incompatible with the mission to establish a peace-loving democratic society. With the postwar economic recovery and continued prosperity, however, Bushido's reputation was resurrected and it was touted once again as being the essential source of Japan's national vitality. Success in the world of sports, business and most other things nowadays is attributed to the "spirit of Bushido," and failure or decadence blamed on a lack of it.

Inazō Nitobe's Bushido

Published in 1900, Inazō's *Bushido: The Soul of Japan* was long considered in the West as the foremost guide into the mind of the Japanese. After the Russo-Japanese War, the book was translated into dozens of languages and became an international bestseller. It is said that even US president Theodore Roosevelt purchased sixty copies to give to friends and family. In 1901, the Japanese publisher Shōkabō entered into an agreement with Inazō to print and sell an English version solely for the Japanese market. The book went through nine printings before Inazō realized the company was fraudulently mass-producing his work. However, the book did help establish his reputation in Japan as a remarkable English language virtuoso and a learned scholar of Japanese ethics. The first Japanese translation, however, only appeared in books stores in 1908.

Although the Japanese were generally gratified at how Inazō's book had made Bushido an internationally recognized word, the domestic Bushido propaganda machine was already in full swing before this. Books and articles by scholars on the relevance of samurai culture and ideology in the modern age had become commonplace. Tokyo Imperial University philosophy and ethics professor, Tetsujirō Inoue, was a prolific writer on the subject and took offence at Inazō's foray into the field, accusing him of "Christianizing" Japan's hallowed culture. Although lay readers were none the wiser, experts in Japanese history were quick to attack Inazō's portrayal of the samurai as being too idealistic and removed from reality. Detractors pointed out that it depicted more a British public-school ethos in samurai clothing, and that it quoted from Western sources rather than authentic works written by samurai themselves. Basil Chamberlain Hall was particularly unforgiving:

> "As for Bushido, so modern a thing is it that neither Kæmpfer, Siebold, Satow, nor Rein—all men knowing their Japan by heart—ever once allude to it in their voluminous writings. The cause of their silence is not far to seek: Bushido was unknown until a decade or two ago! The very word appears in no dictionary, native or foreign, before the year 1900.... The accounts given of it have been fabricated out of whole cloth, chiefly for foreign consumption." (*The Invention of a New Religion*, 1912)

As if anticipating this criticism, in an essay called "Samuraism: The Moral Ideas of Japan" (1901) Inazō wrote:

> "If Christianity teaches us to be stewards of our wealth, Bushido taught us to be stewards of our health; and if Christianity teaches that our body is the temple of the Holy Ghost, Bushido learned from Shintoism that in our tenement of clay is a divine immanence. I do not mean by this that Bushido was deistic, much less can I affirm that it was monotheistic. It was too naive and too unsophisticated to invent a theological system." (*Thoughts and Essays*, p. 334)

One of the striking features of Inazō's book, and indeed all his work, is the eloquent prose he uses to express his ideas. Some commentators have accused Inazō of using "flowery" language to camouflage his flawed knowledge, but I believe it was the product of the countless hours he spent in libraries perfecting his linguistic ability by absorbing and memorizing the greatest and most sophisticated examples of English literature.

Inazō's book begins with an explanation of the origins of Bushido and how it was imbued with teachings from Shinto, Buddhist and Confucian thought. He explains the seven virtues inherent in the warrior's code: rectitude, courage, benevolence, politeness, veracity, honor and loyalty. He talks of how the samurai eschewed matters of commerce, were prepared to die to preserve their honor and would never go back on their word. He also validated the role of the samurai customs of revenge and *seppuku* (ritual suicide), the role of women in samurai society, and how although once exclusively the code of the warrior class it was through popular culture such as theater and literature that these ideals permeated the hearts of the Japanese. This was made possible by the reverence in which the samurai, proponents of *noblesse oblige*, were held by the common people.

Inazō's book is an attempt to promote the idea of Bushido as a benevolent martial code that is neither unlike nor exactly the same as Western chivalry. His intention was to demonstrate that even though Christian morality was not a part of the Japanese psyche, the layers of Bushido can be peeled back to reveal a core that is remarkably similar. In other words, he set forth a universal set of values to clarify to Westerners that the Japanese were by no means backward in terms of their moral outlook. Moreover, the fact that the virtues of Bushido were ingrained in the Japanese people meant that the country was a fertile place to spread the Christian gospel. He did not believe Bushido was the be all and end all, but that it was in line with Thomas Carlyle's *Sartor Resartus*, "Philosophy of Clothes," an unwritten code of ethics and beliefs that was constantly in flux and would pave the way for greater things. A short essay titled "Plebianism" (1904) makes his stance clear:

> "It has been the foundation, the corner-stone, the pillar, of our national morality; but the times are changing, and the samurai are no more, though the precepts which molded their character survive them still. These precepts must find a new application to changed circumstances; they must be democratized. The light which illumed the summit and the breast of society, must now enlighten its broader basis. Shi-do [Way of the warrior gentry] must be transformed into Min-do [Way of the Japanese people], the precepts of the people. With advancing education, bushi, fighting nobles, will recede and heimin (ordinary—or let us rather translate it as peaceful people) must come to the front." (*Thoughts and Essays*, p. 58)

Born into a samurai family at the end of seven centuries of warrior dominance, Inazō was more qualified than most to publish such an exposition. Admittedly, my own scholarly investigations into the history of Bushido have been somewhat critical of his adaptation, and I have in previous writings belittled it as a perfect example of "invented tradition." I submit here, however, that the imperative of academic hypothesizing has blinded me to the obvious beauty of his work by treating "invented tradition" as inferior. All tradition is invented at some time. Musashi Miyamoto's *Book of Five Rings* (1645) promotes his personal principles of strategy and way of life forged through actual combat experience. Jōchō Yamamoto's *Hagakure* (1716) espouses an existentialist samurai ethos peculiar and pertinent to dispirited warriors of the Saga domain. Yūzan Daidōji's *Budō Shoshinshū* (1711) paints a homogenous warrior philosophy, a cosmopolitan samurai *raison d'être* to circumvent confrontation and uphold the law in a time of peace.

These too, are all "invented traditions" pertinent to a specific time, region and people, and to political and social circumstances. What makes these versions more authentic than Inazō's interpretation of Bushido?

There is no such thing as a definitive canon of Bushido, just a whole lot of different ideals associated with the lifestyles and needs of samurai. Therein lies the problem with Inazō's Bushido or, more precisely, the way others perceive his Bushido as *the* definitive account. It is not, and neither did Inazō intend it to be; but the climate was perfect for his book to exceed all expectations and capture the imagination of people everywhere. As an entry for understanding the complexities of Japan, it was a timely masterpiece.

Inazō Nitobe was born a samurai. His early childhood education infused in him an attitude and a moral compass that formed the bedrock of his character. Various forms of the warrior ideal have always existed in Japan. However, as I have suggested above, there was a common ideological thread connecting them through the vicissitudes of time: honor was gained and sustained through steadfastness in service, wholesomeness in thought and wholeheartedness in action. The magnificence of Inazō's rendering of Bushido lies in how he takes cues from a mélange of spiritual traditions and philosophies and weaves them through the filaments of his samurai upbringing into a timeless and universal monument of human virtue. To this day, Inazō's Bushido represents an inspiring expansion of various traditional virtues remolded to guide modern sensibilities amidst times of monumental change.

Year	Inazō Nitobe Chronology	Historical Episode
1862	Born in Morioka on September 1 to a samurai family which served the Nanbu lord. Was named Inanosuke.	
1867	Father Jūjirō Nitobe dies.	**Meiji Restoration 1868:** Restoration of imperial rule proclaimed by samurai rebels. Boshin War ensues and the shogunate is replaced after seven centuries of warrior rule.
1871	Grandfather Tsutō Nitobe dies. Is sent to Tokyo with his brother Michirō to live with their uncle, Tokitoshi Ōta. Change their surnames from Nitobe to Ōta.	
1872	Enters private English school in Tokyo.	**Class Distinctions Dismantled 1869:** *Shi* (samurai), *nō* (farmer), *kō* (artisan) and *shō* (merchant) replaced by three broad categories: *kazoku* (former court nobles and *daimyō*), *shizoku* (those of samurai descent) and *heimin* (commoners). Domains replaced with prefectures.
1873	Enters Tokyo School of Foreign Languages (later Tokyo English School).	
1876	Emperor Meiji stays at the Nitobe second home in Sanbongi.	
1877	Attends Sapporo Agricultural College (SAC), a newly established, nationally funded school, with his friends Kanzō Uchimura and Kingo Miyabe. Signs the "Covenant of Believers in Jesus" at SAC and becomes a Christian.	**Danpatsu Rei 1871:** Ordinance instructing former samurai to remove their topknots. **Conscription Ordinance 1873:** All males undergo military training, which used to be the domain of samurai only. **Sword Ban Order 1876:** No longer legal to wear swords in public unless a military or police officer. **Satsuma Rebellion 1877**
1880	Mother Seki dies. Reads Thomas Carlyle's *Sartor Restarus* (1836) for the first time.	

Year	Inazō Nitobe Chronology	Historical Episode
1881	Graduates from SAC. Works for the Hokkaido Colonization Office.	
1883	Enters Tokyo Imperial University to study economics and English literature.	
1884	Withdraws from Tokyo Imperial University in August. Travels to the United States and enters Johns Hopkins University to study history and political science.	
1886	Joins the Society of Friends (Quakers) in Philadelphia. Meets Mary Elkinton.	
1887	Leaves America for Germany in May. Studies at the University of Bonn.	
1888	Studies at the University of Berlin.	
1889	Commences study at the University of Halle. Reverts back to Nitobe surname from Ōta.	
1890	Visits America in October on his way back to Japan.	
1891	Marries Mary Elkinton in Philadelphia on January 1. Returns to Sapporo to take up a teaching post at SAC.	
1892	Son Thomas is born but dies a week later.	
1893	Publishes *The Imperial Agricultural College of Sapporo* for the Chicago World Expo.	

Year	Inazō Nitobe Chronology	Historical Episode
1894	Publishes a biography of William Penn in Japanese.	**First Sino-Japanese War 1894–95**
1895	Establishes the Friends from Afar Night School in Sapporo.	Taiwan becomes Japan's first colony.
1897	Resigns from SAC in October due to poor health.	
1898	Travels to California with Mary to convalesce.	
1899	**Writes Bushido: The Soul of Japan in Monterey.**	
1900	**Bushido: The Soul of Japan is published by Leeds & Biddle in Philadelphia in January.**	
1901	Begins work as an administrator of the Taiwan Government House. Tours the Philippines, Java and Australia.	
1902	Contributes to developing the lucrative sugar industry in Taiwan, which becomes the fourth largest exporter of sugar in the world.	
1903	Appointed Professor of Law (colonial policy) at Kyoto Imperial University.	**Russo-Japanese War 1904–05** The southern half of Karafuto is acquired by Japan. Lease of the Guandong Territory is transferred from Russia to Japan, together with the right to control the South Manchuria Railway.
1906	Appointed Headmaster of the First Higher School in Tokyo.	
1909	Editorial adviser for *Jitsugyō no Nihon* magazine. Appointed Professor of Law at Tokyo Imperial University. Publishes *Thoughts and Essays*.	**Korean Annexation (1910)**
1911	Exchange professor at six universities in the US.	

Year	Inazō Nitobe Chronology	Historical Episode
1912	Publishes *The Japanese Nation*.	**Meiji Emperor Dies. Beginning of Taishō Period**
1913	Retires from the First Higher School.	**World War I 1914–18**
1918	Becomes president of the newly established Tokyo Women's Christian College.	
1920	Appointed Under-Secretary-General to the League of Nations.	
1922	Helps establish the International Committee for Intellectual Cooperation (forerunner to UNESCO).	**American Immigration Act 1924** **Shōwa Period 1926–89**
1926	Retires from the League of Nations. Receives imperial appointment as a member of the House of Peers.	
1927	Returns to Japan on March 16. Publishes *Japanese Traits and Foreign Influences*.	
1929	Becomes Chairman of the IPR Japan Council. Attends conference in Kyoto.	**Great Depression**
1930	Editorial adviser to *Osaka Mainichi* newspaper.	
1931	Attends the IPR conference in Shanghai.	**Manchurian Incident:** The conquest and pacification of Manchuria by Japan's field army in Manchuria, from September 1931 to January 1933, starting with an attack on the Chinese garrison in Mukden on the night of September 18–19, 1931.

Year	Inazō Nitobe Chronology	Historical Episode
1932	Criticism of militarism is reported in the newspaper (Matsuyama Incident). Forced to apologize to the nationalistic veteran association. Departs for a lecture tour of the US on April 14.	**Shanghai Incident:** Military confrontation between Chinese and Japanese troops in Shanghai from 28 January to May 5, 1932. **May 15 Incident:** Attempted coup d'état by young naval officers on May 15, 1932. Their assassination of Prime Minister Tsuyoshi Inukai led to the demise of the party cabinet system.
1933	Returns to Japan on March 25. Leaves for the IPR conference in Banff, Canada. **Dies in the Royal Jubilee Hospital, Victoria, Canada, on October 15.**	**League of Nations Withdrawal** Japan notifies the League of its withdrawal on March 27, 1933 in response to the Lytton Commission report condemning Japan's military action in Manchuria.

References

Bennett, Alexander C., *Hagakure: The Secret Wisdom of the Samurai*, Vermont: Tuttle, 2014.

_____, *Kendo: Culture of the Sword*, Berkeley: University of California Press, 2015.

Howes, John F., *Japan's Modern Prophet: Uchimura Kanzō, 1861–1930*, Vancouver: University of British Columbia Press, 2005.

_____, *Nitobe Inazo: Japan's Bridge Across the Pacific*, Boulder, CO: Westview Press, 1995.

Iglehart, Charles A., *A Century of Protestant Christianity in Japan*, Tokyo: Charles E. Tuttle, 1959.

Kageyama Reiko, *Naruse Jinzō no kyōiku shisō*, Tokyo: Kazama Shobō, 1994.

Kawabata Takashi, Ohnishi Naoki and Nishide Kimiyuki (eds.), *W. S. Clark's Letters from Japan*, Sapporo: Miyama Press, 1987.

Li Tō Ki, *Bushidō Kaidai*, Tokyo: Shōgakkan, 2003.

Matsukuma Toshiko, *Nitobe Inazō*, Tokyo: Misuzu Shobō, 1969.

Morris-Suzuki, Tessa, *Re-Inventing Japan: Time, Space, Nation*, Armonk, NY and London: M. E. Sharpe, 1998.

Nagao Teruhiko (ed.), *Nitobe Inazō: From Bushido to the League of Nations*, Sapporo: Graduate School of Letters, Hokkaido University, 2006.

Naramoto Tatsuya, *Bushidō no Keifu*, Tokyo: Chūō Kōronsha, 1971.

_____ (trans.), *Gendaigo de yomu Saikō no Meicho: Bushidō*, Tokyo: Mikasa Shobō, 1993.

Nitobe Inazō, *Nitobe Inazō Zenshū*, Tokyo: Kyōbunkan, 1984 (reprint of vols. 1–16 originally published 1969–70; vols. 17–23 originally published 1985–87).

Oshiro, George Masaaki, "Internationalist in Prewar Japan: Nitobe Inazō, 1862–1933)," unpublished Ph.D. thesis, University of British Columbia, 1985.

_____, "Nitobe and Nationalism," in Roy Starrs (ed.), *Japanese Cultural Nationalism: At Home and in the Asia Pacific*, London: Global Oriental, 2003, pp. 61–79.

Ōta Yūzō, *Taiheiyō no Hashi Toshite no Nitobe Inazō*, Tokyo: Misuzu Shobo, 1986.

Satō Masahiro (trans.), *Bushido: The Soul of Japan*, Tokyo: Kyōbunkan, 2000.

Yamamoto Hirofumi, *Nitobe Inazō: Bushidō*, Tokyo: NHK Books, 2012.

Introduction

At the request of his publishers, to whom Dr. Nitobe has left some freedom of action concerning prefatory matter, I am glad to offer a few sentences of introduction to this new edition of Bushido, for readers of English everywhere. I have been acquainted with the author for over fifteen years, indeed, but, in a measure at least, with his subject during forty-five years.

It was in 1860, in Philadelphia (where, in 1847, I saw the *Susquehanna*, Commodore Perry's[1] flagship launched), that I looked on my first Japanese and met members of the Embassy from Yedo.[2] I was mightily impressed with these strangers, to whom Bushido was a living code of ideals and manners. Later, during three years at Rutgers College, New Brunswick, N.J., I was among scores of young men from Nippon, whom I taught or knew as fellow-students. I found that Bushido, about which we often talked, was a superbly winsome thing. As illustrated in the lives of these future governors, diplomatists, admirals, educators, and bankers, yes, even in the dying hours of more than one who "fell on sleep"[3] in Willow Grove

---

[1] Commodore Matthew Calbraith Perry (1794–1858), an American naval officer credited with opening Japan to the Western world after more than 200 years of "National Isolation." He was commissioned in 1852 to sail to Japan and negotiate the commencement of diplomatic and commercial relations. Arriving on July 8, 1853 in Edo Bay with his ominous "Black Ships," this first official contact between Japan and the United States eventually led to the securing of treaties to open ports.

[2] Edo, or modern-day Tokyo.

[3] A biblical euphemism for dying.

Cemetery,[4] the perfume of this most fragrant flower of far-off Japan was very sweet. Never shall I forget how the dying samurai lad, Kusakabe, when invited to the noblest of services and the greatest of hopes, made answer: "Even if I could know your Master, Jesus, I should not offer Him only the dregs of a life." So, "on the banks of the old Raritan,"[5] in athletic sports, in merry jokes at the supper table when contrasting things Japanese and Yankee, and in the discussion of ethics and ideals, I felt quite willing to take the "covert missionary retort," about which my friend Charles Dudley Warner once wrote.[6] At some points, codes of ethics and proprieties differed, but rather in dots or tangents than as occultation or eclipse. As their own poet wrote—was it a thousand years ago?—when in crossing a moor the dew-laden flowers brushed by his robe left their glittering drops on his brocade, "On account of its perfume, I brush not this moisture from my sleeve."[7] Indeed, I was glad to get out of ruts, which are said to differ from graves only by their length. For, is not comparison the life of science and culture? Is it not true that, in the study of languages, ethics, religions, and codes of manners, "he who knows but one knows none"?[8]

---

[4] The Willow Grove Cemetery in New Brunswick, New Jersey, is the burial place of several of the first Japanese exchange students who studied in the United States. The man mentioned here is Tarō Kusakabe (1845–70), a young samurai from Fukui and a student of William Elliot Griffis at Rutgers University. Kusakabe died of tuberculosis and was awarded his degree posthumously.

[5] The Raritan is a major river of central New Jersey and is mentioned in a verse in Rutgers University's hymn.

[6] Charles Dudley Warner (1829–1900), an American writer and a friend of Mark Twain with whom he co-authored the novel *The Gilded Age: A Tale of Today*. The phrase "covert missionary retort" could have come from *An Artist's Letters from Japan* (1897) by John La Farge (1835–1910). "Those [samurai] who lived under the ideals of *noblesse oblige* adorn the annals of Japan, and are the fathers of those young men who in Europe and America have given us 'a covert missionary retort' by their gentleness, winsome politeness, and fine mental traits" (p. 236).

[7] Possibly poem 224 from the ancient anthology *Kokinshū*.

[8] A reference to the ideals of British scholar Max Müller (1823–1900). Müller

Called, in 1870, to Japan as pioneer educator to introduce the
methods and spirit of the American public-school system, how
glad I was to leave the capital, and at Fukui, in the province of
Echizen, see pure feudalism in operation! There I looked on Bushido, not as an exotic, but in its native soil. In daily life I realized
that Bushido, with its *cha-no-yu, jū-jŭtsŭ* ("jiu-jutsu") *hara-kiri,*[9]
polite prostrations on the mats and genuflections[10] on the street,
rules of the sword and road, all leisurely salutations and politest
molds of speech, canons of art and conduct, as well as heroisms for
wife, maid, and child, formed the universal creed and praxis of all
the gentry in the castled city and province. In it, as a living school
of thought and life, girl and boy alike were trained. What Dr. Nitobe received as an inheritance, had breathed into his nostrils, and
writes about so gracefully and forcibly, with such grasp, insight, and
breadth of view, I saw. Japanese feudalism "died without the sight"
of its ablest exponent and most convincing defender.[11] To him it is
as wafted fragrance. To me it was "the plant and flower of light."[12]

Hence, living under and being in at the death of feudalism, the
body of Bushido, I can bear witness to the essential truth of Dr. Nitobe's descriptions, so far as they go, and to the faithfulness of his
analysis and generalizations. He has limned with masterly art and
reproduced the coloring of the picture which a thousand years of
Japanese literature reflects so gloriously. The Knightly Code grew
up during a millennium of evolution, and our author lovingly notes
the blooms that have starred the path trodden by millions of noble

---

was of the opinion that religious traditions were best understood through comparing their doctrines and methods.

[9] Tea ceremony, martial arts and ritual disembowelment respectively.

[10] A gesture of deep respect to a superior by kneeling on one or both knees.

[11] This is a phrase used in Christianity with regards to people who are resolved
in their faith that the Messiah will arise once more, but do not live to see the
prophecy come true.

[12] Cited from a poem by Ben Jonson (1573–1637), "To the Immortal Memory
and Friendship of that noble pair, Sir Lucius Cary and Sir H. Morison" (1629).

souls, his countrymen.

Critical study has but deepened my own sense of the potency and value of Bushido to the nation. He who would understand twentieth-century Japan must know something of its roots in the soil of the past. Even if now as invisible to the present generation in Nippon[13] as to the alien, the philosophic student reads the results of today in the stored energies of ages gone. The sunbeams of unrecorded time have laid the strata out of which Japan now digs her foot-pounds of impact for war or peace. All the spiritual senses are keen in those nursed by Bushido. The crystalline lump has dissolved in the sweetened cup, but the delicacy of the flavor remains to cheer. In a word, Bushido has obeyed the higher law enunciated by One whom its own exponent salutes and confesses his Master—"Except a grain of corn die, it abideth alone; but if it die it bringeth forth much fruit."[14]

Has Dr. Nitobe idealized Bushido? Rather, we ask, how could he help doing so? He calls himself "defendant." In all creeds, cults, and systems, while the ideal grows, exemplars and exponents vary. Gradual cumulation and slow attainment of harmony is the law. Bushido never reached a final goal. It was too much alive, and it died at last only in its splendor and strength. The clash of the world's movement—for so we name the rush of influences and events which followed Perry and Harris[15]—with feudalism in Japan, did not find Bushido an embalmed mummy, but a living soul.

---

[13] Japan.

[14] John 12:24–26. Jesus uses the allegory of wheat to highlight that humility is of great consequence in seeking salvation. In other words, believers must purge themselves of worldly preconceptions to become a stronger, more virtuous person.

[15] Townsend Harris (1804–78) served as the first American Consul General in Japan. He arrived in 1856 on a mission to secure an agreement allowing full commercial activities with Japan. He left in 1862 after successfully negotiating the United States–Japan Treaty of Amity and Commerce, which took effect from 1859.

What it really met was the quickening spirit of humanity. Then the less was blessed of the greater. Without losing the best in her own history and civilization, Japan, following her own noble precedents, first adopted and then adapted the choicest the world had to offer. Thus her opportunity to bless Asia and the race became unique, and grandly she has embraced it—"in diffusion ever more intense."[16] Today, not only are our gardens, our art, our homes enriched by the flowers, the pictures, and the pretty things of Japan, whether "trifles of a moment or triumphs for all time," but in physical culture, in public hygiene, in lessons for peace and war, Japan has come to us with her hands gift-laden.

Not only in his discourse as advocate and counsel for the defense, but as prophet and wise householder, rich in things new and old, our author is able to teach us. No man in Japan has united the precepts and practice of his own Bushido more harmoniously in life and toil, labor and work, craft of hand and of pen, culture of the soil and of the soul. Illuminator of Dai Nippon's past, Dr. Nitobe is a true maker of the New Japan. In Formosa,[17] the empire's new accretion, as in Kioto,[18] he is the scholar and practical man, at home in newest science and most ancient diligence.

This little book on Bushido is more than a weighty message to the Anglo-Saxon nations. It is a notable contribution to the solution of this century's grandest problem—the reconciliation and unity of the East and the West. There were of many old civilizations: in the better world coming there will be one. Already the terms "Ori-

---

[16] From a poem by George Eliot (1819–80), "Oh May I Join the Choir Invisible" (1867).

[17] Taiwan. Nitobe was appointed as an advisor to the Japanese colonial government of Taiwan in 1901. Specializing in agronomy, his reform plans to expand sugar production in the colony resulted in a six-fold increase in one decade. This further increased to over forty-fold in two decades. Partly because of this achievement he became a professor in the Law Faculty at Kyoto Imperial University.

[18] Kyoto.

ent" and "Occident," with all their freight of mutual ignorance and insolence, are ready to pass away. As the efficient middle term between the wisdom and communism[19] of Asia and the energy and individualism of Europe and America, Japan is already working with resistless power.

Instructed in things ancient and modern and cultured in the literatures of the world, Dr. Nitobe herein shows himself admirably fitted for a congenial task. He is a true interpreter and reconciler. He need not and does not apologize for his own attitude toward the Master whom he has long loyally followed. What scholar, familiar with the ways of the Spirit and with the history of the race as led by man's Infinite Friend, but must in all religions put difference between the teachings of the Founder and the original documents and the ethnic, rationalistic, and ecclesiastical additions and accretions?[20] The doctrine of the testaments, hinted at in the author's preface, is the teaching of Him who came not to destroy, but to fulfill. Even in Japan, Christianity, unwrapped from its foreign mold and matting, will cease being an exotic and strike its roots deep in the soil on which Bushido has grown. Stripped alike of its swaddling bands and its foreign regimentals, the church of the Founder will be as native as the air.

William Elliot Griffis[21]
Ithaca, May 1905

---

[19] Not Marxian Communism or the like, but the notion of groupism where people are viewed as members of a collective rather than as individuals.

[20] Growth in size or extent.

[21] William Elliot Griffis (1843–1928), a prominent Philadelphia-born educator and clergyman and prolific author of things Japanese. As he alludes to in his introduction, Griffis tutored several of the first Japanese students to study in the United States when he was a student at Rutgers University (1865–69). After graduation, he came to Japan in 1870 and taught chemistry and physics at the invitation of the Fukui domain, and later at the forerunner of Tokyo University until 1874 when he returned to the United States.

That way Over the mountain, which who stands upon
Is apt to doubt if it be indeed a road;
While if he views it from the waste itself,
Up goes the line there, plain from base to brow,
Not vague, mistakable!
What's a break or two Seen from the unbroken deserts either side?
And then (to bring in fresh philosophy)
What if the breaks themselves should prove at last
The most consummate of contrivances
To train a man's eye, teach him what is faith?

Robert Browning
Bishop Blougram's Apology

There are, if I may so say, three powerful spirits, which have, from
time to time, moved on the face of the waters, and given a predom-
inant impulse to the moral sentiments and energies of mankind.
These are the spirits of liberty, of religion, and of honor.

Hallam
Europe in the Middle Ages

Chivalry is itself the poetry of life.

Schlegel
Philosophy of History

CHAPTER I

Bushido as an Ethical System

C hivalry is a flower no less indigenous to the soil of Japan than its emblem, the cherry blossom; nor is it a dried-up specimen of an antique virtue preserved in the herbarium[1] of our history. It is still a living object of power and beauty among us, and if it assumes no tangible shape or form, it none the less scents the moral atmosphere and makes us aware that we are still under its potent spell. The conditions of society which brought it forth and nourished it have long disappeared; but as those far-off stars which once were and are not, still continue to shed their rays upon us, so the light of chivalry, which was a child of feudalism, still illuminates our moral path, surviving its mother institution. It is a pleasure to me to reflect upon this subject in the language of Burke,[2] who uttered the well-known touching eulogy over the neglected bier[3] of its European prototype.

It argues a sad defect of information concerning the Far East, when so erudite a scholar as Dr. George Miller[4] did not hesitate to

---

[1] A building or room where plant specimens are housed.

[2] Edmund Burke (1730–97), an Irish statesman, author and philosopher. He was a stickler for good manners and a vocal proponent of the crucial role religion played in nurturing morality.

[3] A bier is a stand on which a corpse, coffin or casket is placed.

[4] George Miller (1764–1848), an Irish Anglican priest and assistant professor at Trinity College, Dublin. Miller's lectures on history were published in eight parts

affirm that chivalry, or any other similar institution, has never existed either among the nations of antiquity or among the modern Orientals.[5] Such ignorance, however, is amply excusable, as the third edition of the good Doctor's work appeared the same year that Commodore Perry was knocking at the portals of our exclusivism.[6] More than a decade later, about the time that our feudalism was in the last throes of existence, Karl Marx, writing his *Kapital*, called the attention of his readers to the peculiar advantage of studying the social and political institutions of feudalism, as then to be seen in living form only in Japan. I would likewise point the Western historical and ethical student to the study of chivalry in the Japan of the present.

Enticing as is an historical disquisition[7] on the comparison between European and Japanese feudalism[8] and chivalry, it is not the purpose of this paper to enter into it at length. My attempt is rather to relate firstly, the origin and sources of our chivalry; secondly, its character and teaching; thirdly, its influence among the masses; and, fourthly, the continuity and permanence of its influence. Of

---

as the acclaimed body of work, *History Philosophically Illustrated, from the Fall of the Roman Empire, to the French Revolution*.

[5] [*History Philosophically Illustrated* (3rd edn, 1853), vol. ii, p. 2.]

[6] Nitobe is referring to the Tokugawa shogunate-initiated policy of "National Isolation" (*Sakoku*). Lasting from 1639 to 1854, this law prohibited foreign travel by Japanese and prevented foreigners from freely coming to Japan. The main exception were the Dutch who were the only Westerners allowed to set up a trading post, albeit on a tiny island called Dejima in Nagasaki.

[7] A formal inquiry into or discussion of a subject.

[8] Depending on the era, several characteristics of the social and political systems implemented in pre-modern Japan resemble European feudalism. For example, in Japan as in Europe there was an agriculture-based economy, a dominant class of warriors bound by ties of fealty and the rewarding of fiefs, and an established warrior elite ethos that exalted virtues of valor, honor, loyalty and so on. Nevertheless, there were also many important differences. For example, vassalage networks in Japan were much simpler than in Europe, where knights were known to become vassals of several lords simultaneously in order to claim more fiefdoms.

these several points, the first will be only brief and cursory, or else I should have to take my readers into the devious paths of our national history; the second will be dwelt upon at greater length, as being most likely to interest students of International Ethics and Comparative Ethnology in our ways of thought and action; and the rest will be dealt with as corollaries.

The Japanese word which I have roughly rendered as Chivalry is, in the original, more expressive than Horsemanship.[9] *Bu-shi-do* means literally Military-Knight-Ways—the ways which fighting nobles should observe in their daily life as well as in their vocation; in a word, the "Precepts of Knighthood," the *noblesse oblige*[10] of the warrior class. Having thus given its literal significance, I may be allowed henceforth to use the word in the original. The use of the original term is also advisable for this reason, that a teaching so circumscribed and unique, engendering a cast of mind and character so peculiar, so local, must wear the badge of its singularity on its face; then, some words have a national timbre so expressive of race characteristics that the best of translators can do them but scant justice, not to say positive injustice and grievance. Who can improve by translation what the German "Gemüth"[11] signifies, or who does not feel the difference between the two words verbally so closely allied as the English gentleman and the French *gentilhomme*?

Bushido, then, is the code of moral principles which the knights were required or instructed to observe. It is not a written code; at best it consists of a few maxims handed down from mouth to mouth or coming from the pen of some well-known warrior or savant. More frequently it is a code unuttered and unwritten, possessing all the more the powerful sanction of veritable deed, and of a law written on the fleshly tablets of the heart. It was founded not

---

[9] "Chivalry" originally meant "horsemanship."

[10] A French phrase meaning the obligation of honorable and responsible behavior associated with persons of high rank or birth.

[11] A term meaning heart, mind, temper or mood.

on the creation of one brain, however able, or on the life of a single personage, however renowned. It was an organic growth of decades and centuries of military career. It, perhaps, fills the same position in the history of ethics that the English Constitution does in political history; yet it has had nothing to compare with the Magna Carta[12] or the Habeas Corpus Act.[13] True, early in the seventeenth century Military Statutes (*Buké Hatto*)[14] were promulgated; but their thirteen short articles were taken up mostly with marriages, castles, leagues, etc., and didactic regulations were but meagerly touched upon. We cannot, therefore, point out any definite time and place and say, "Here is its fountainhead." Only as it attains consciousness in the feudal age, its origin, in respect to time, may be identified with feudalism. But feudalism itself is woven of many threads, and Bushido shares its intricate nature. As in England the political institutions of feudalism may be said to date from the Norman Conquest,[15] so we may say that in Japan its rise was simultaneous with the ascendancy of Yoritomo,[16] late in the twelfth century. As, however, in England, we find the social elements of feudalism far back in the period previous to William the Conqueror, so, too,

---

[12] The Magna Carta was a charter agreed to by King John of England in 1215 to placate rebellious barons. King John consented to the protection of church rights, desisting from unwarranted imprisonment, and a reduction of mandatory payments to the crown. It became an established part of English politics to guarantee the protection of individual freedoms.

[13] The Habeas Corpus Act of 1679 was enacted in England during the reign of King Charles II. It required authorities to observe the lawfulness of any individual's detention.

[14] Originally containing thirteen articles, the *Buke Shohatto* (Laws for the Military Houses) was a code of conduct issued by the Tokugawa shogunate (1603–1867) in 1615. A catalogue of prohibited behavior, the *Buke Shohatto* was more symbolic than directorial.

[15] The military conquest of England by William the Conqueror of Normandy after his pivotal victory at the Battle of Hastings (1066).

[16] Minamoto-no-Yoritomo (1147–99), the founder of Japan's first warrior government, the Kamakura shogunate (1192–1333).

the germs of feudalism in Japan had been long existent before the period I have mentioned.

Again, in Japan as in Europe, when feudalism was formally inaugurated, the professional class of warriors naturally came into prominence. These were known as *samurai*, meaning literally, like the old English *cniht* (knecht, knight), guards, or attendants—resembling in character the *soldurii*, whom Caesar mentioned as existing in Aquitania,[17] or the *comitati*, who, according to Tacitus,[18] followed Germanic chiefs in his time; or, to take a still later parallel, the *milites medii* that one reads about in the history of Medieval Europe. The Sinico-Japanese[19] words *Bu-ké or Bu-shi* (Fighting Knights) were also adopted in common use. They were a privileged class and must originally have been a rough breed who made fighting their vocation. This class was naturally recruited, in a long period of constant warfare, from the manliest and the most adventurous, and all the while the process of elimination went on, the timid and the feeble being sorted out, and only "a rude race, all masculine, with brutish strength," to borrow Emerson's[20] phrase, surviving to form families and the ranks of the samurai. Coming to profess great honor and great privileges, and correspondingly great responsibilities, they soon felt the need of a common standard of behavior, especially as they were always on a belligerent footing and belonged to different clans. Just as physicians limit competition among themselves by professional courtesy, just as lawyers sit in

---

[17] Gallia Aquitania was a province of the Roman Empire located in present-day southwest France.

[18] Publius (or Gaius) Cornelius Tacitus (c. AD 56–c. 120), a senator and prominent historian of the Roman Empire.

[19] Sino-Japanese.

[20] Ralph Waldo Emerson (1803–82), an American essayist and poet who led the transcendentalist movement of the mid-nineteenth century. He believed in the inherent goodness of people and nature, and that society and its trappings exerted corrupting influences on the individual. Quoted from his *English Traits* (1856).

courts of honor in cases of violated etiquette; so must also warriors possess some resort for final judgment on their misdemeanors.

Fair play in fight! What fertile germs of morality lie in this primitive sense of savagery and childhood. Is it not the root of all military and civic virtue? We smile (as if we had outgrown it!) at the boyish desire of the small Britisher, Tom Brown, "to leave behind him the name of a fellow who never bullied a little boy or turned his back on a big one."[21] And yet, who does not know that this desire is the cornerstone on which moral structures of mighty dimensions can be reared? May I not go even so far as to say that the gentlest and most peace-loving of religions endorses this aspiration? The desire of Tom is the basis on which the greatness of England is largely built, and it will not take us long to discover that Bushido does not stand on a lesser pedestal. If fighting in itself, be it offensive or defensive, is, as Quakers[22] rightly testify, brutal and wrong, we can still say with Lessing,[23] "We know from what failings our virtue springs."[24] "Sneaks" and "cowards" are epithets of

---

[21] Tom Brown is a fictional character in Thomas Hughes's *Tom Brown's School Days* (1857). Set in the Rugby School for Boys in 1830s England, it centers on the trials and tribulations of growing up and contending with bullies in an institution steeped in tradition.

[22] Quakers are members of the Society of Friends, a Christian religious movement united in the idea that all humans can access "the small light within." In other words, it is a belief that God is in all people.

[23] Gotthold Ephraim Lessing (1729–81), a German writer, philosopher, dramatist and art critic whose contributions to the Enlightenment and influence on German literature were profound. Quoted from his play "*Nathan the Wise*" (1779).

[24] [Ruskin was one of the most gentle-hearted and peace-loving men that ever lived. Yet he believed in war with all the fervor of a worshipper of the strenuous life. "When I tell you," he says in the *Crown of Wild Olive*, "that war is the foundation of all the arts, I mean also that it is the foundation of all the high virtues and faculties of men. It is very strange to me to discover this, and very dreadful, but I saw it to be quite an undeniable fact.... I found, in brief, that all great nations learned their truth of word and strength of thought in war; that they were nourished in war and wasted by peace; taught by war and deceived by peace;

the worst opprobrium[25] to healthy, simple natures.

Childhood begins life with these notions, and knighthood also, but, as life grows larger and its relations many-sided, the early faith seeks sanction from higher authority and more rational sources for its own justification, satisfaction, and development. If military systems had operated alone, without higher moral support, how far short of chivalry would the ideal of knighthood have fallen! In Europe, Christianity, interpreted with concessions convenient to chivalry, infused it nevertheless with spiritual data. "Religion, war, and glory were the three souls of a perfect Christian knight," says Lamartine.[26] In Japan there were several sources of Bushido.

---

trained by war and betrayed by peace; in a word, that they were born in war and expired in peace."]

[25] Something that brings disgrace.

[26] Alphonse de Lamartine (1790–1869), a French poet and statesman and one of the central figures of the Romantic movement in French literature with his publication *Méditations Poétiques* (1820).

CHAPTER II

Sources of Bushido

I may begin with Buddhism. It furnished a sense of calm trust in Fate, a quiet submission to the inevitable, that stoic composure in sight of danger or calamity, that disdain of life and friendliness with death. A foremost teacher of swordsmanship,[1] when he saw his pupil master the utmost of his art, told him, "Beyond this my instruction must give way to Zen teaching." "Zen" is the Japanese equivalent for the Dhyâna, which "represents human effort to reach through meditation zones of thought beyond the range of verbal expression."[2] Its method is contemplation, and its purport, so far as I understand it, to be convinced of a principle that underlies all phenomena, and, if it can, of the Absolute[3] itself, and thus to put oneself in harmony with this Absolute. Thus defined, the teaching was more than the dogma of a sect, and whoever attains to the perception of the Absolute raises himself above mundane things and awakes "to a new Heaven and a new Earth."

What Buddhism failed to give, Shintoism[4] offered in abundance. Such loyalty to the sovereign, such reverence for ancestral memory, and such filial piety as are not taught by any other creed,

---

[1] Yagyū Munenori (1571–1646), a famous swordsman of the early Edo period. He taught Yagyū Shinkage-ryū swordsmanship to three generations of Tokugawa shoguns and wrote the influential *Heihō Kadensho* (1632), a treatise connecting principles of swordsmanship with governance.

[2] [Lafcadio Hearn, *Exotics and Retrospectives*, p. 84.]

[3] The "truest reality," or the "first and greatest being." God.

[4] The indigenous religion of Japan.

were inculcated by the Shinto doctrines, imparting passivity to the otherwise arrogant character of the samurai. Shinto theology has no place for the dogma of "original sin." On the contrary, it believes in the innate goodness and Godlike purity of the human soul, adoring it as the adytum[5] from which divine oracles are proclaimed. Everybody has observed that the Shinto shrines are conspicuously devoid of objects and instruments of worship, and that a plain mirror hung in the sanctuary forms the essential part of its furnishing. The presence of this article is easy to explain: it typifies the human heart, which, when perfectly placid and clear, reflects the very image of the Deity. When you stand, therefore, in front of the shrine to worship, you see your own image reflected on its shining surface, and the act of worship is tantamount to the old Delphic injunction, "Know Thyself."[6] But self-knowledge does not imply, either in the Greek or Japanese teaching, knowledge of the physical part of man, not his anatomy or his psychophysics; knowledge was to be of a moral kind, the introspection of our moral nature. Mommsen,[7] comparing the Greek and the Roman, says that when the former worshipped he raised his eyes to Heaven, for his prayer was contemplation, while the latter veiled his head, for his was reflection. Essentially like the Roman conception of religion, our reflection brought into prominence not so much the moral as the national consciousness of the individual. Its nature-worship endeared the country to our inmost souls, while its ancestor-worship, tracing from lineage to lineage, made the Imperial family the fountainhead of the whole nation. To us the country is more than land and soil

---

[5] The most sacred or reserved part in any place of worship.

[6] The Ancient Greek dictum "Know Thyself" is inscribed in the Temple of Apollo in Delphi. The maxim was philosophized by such luminaries as Socrates and his students.

[7] Christian Matthias Theodor Mommsen (1817–1903), recipient of the Nobel Prize in Literature in 1920, was one of the greatest German classicists of the nineteenth century. Published in three volumes from 1854–56, his monumental work, *History of Rome*, is still cited in contemporary research.

from which to mine gold or to reap grain—it is the sacred abode of
the gods, the spirits of our forefathers: to us the Emperor is more
than the Arch Constable of a *Rechtsstaat*,[8] or even the Patron of a
Culturstaat[9]—he is the bodily representative of Heaven on earth,
blending in his person its power and its mercy.[10] If what M. Boutmy[11] says is true of English royalty—that it "is not only the image of
authority, but the author and symbol of national unity," as I believe
it to be, doubly and trebly may this be affirmed of royalty in Japan.

The tenets of Shintoism cover the two predominating features of
the emotional life of our race—Patriotism and Loyalty. Arthur May
Knapp[12] very truly says: "In Hebrew literature it is often difficult
to tell whether the writer is speaking of God or of the Commonwealth; of Heaven or of Jerusalem; of the Messiah or of the Nation
itself."[13] A similar confusion may be noticed in the nomenclature
of our national faith. I said confusion, because it will be so deemed
by a logical intellect on account of its verbal ambiguity; still, being a
framework of national instinct and race feelings, it never pretends
to systematic philosophy or a rational theology. This religion—or,
is it not more correct to say, the race emotions which this religion

---

[8] A doctrine originating in German jurisprudence usually translated as "rule of
law" or "state based on justice and integrity."

[9] *Kulturstaat* means "civilized nations," "enlightened countries" or "modern nations."

[10] According to Japanese mythology, the emperor is a direct descendant of the
Sun Goddess, Amaterasu Ōmikami. On January 1, 1946, Emperor Hirohito
officially denounced his own divinity. "The ties between Us and Our people
have always stood upon mutual trust and affection. They do not depend upon
mere legends and myths. They are not predicated on the false conception that
the Emperor is divine and that the Japanese people are superior to other races
and fated to rule the world."

[11] [*The English People*, p. 188.] Émile Boutmy (1835–1906) was a French political
scientist and sociologist and the author of *The English People: A Study of Their
Political Psychology* (1901).

[12] Arthur May Knapp (1841–1921), a missionary dispatched on an evangelical
mission to Japan in the late 1880s by the American Unitarian Association.

[13] [*Feudal and Modern Japan*, vol. i, p. 183.]

expressed?—thoroughly imbued Bushido with loyalty to the sovereign and love of country. These acted more as impulses than as doctrines; for Shintoism, unlike the Medieval Christian Church, prescribed to its votaries[14] scarcely any *credenda*,[15] furnishing them at the same time with *agenda* of a straightforward and simple type.

As to strictly ethical doctrines, the teachings of Confucius were the most prolific source of Bushido.[16] His enunciation of the five moral relations between master and servant (the governing and the governed), father and son, husband and wife, older and younger brother, and between friend and friend, was but a confirmation of what the race instinct had recognized before his writings were introduced from China. The calm, benignant,[17] and worldly-wise character of his politico-ethical precepts was particularly well suited to the samurai, who formed the ruling class. His aristocratic and conservative tone was well adapted to the requirements of these warrior statesmen. Next to Confucius, Mencius exercised an immense authority over Bushido. His forcible and often quite democratic theories were exceedingly taking to sympathetic natures, and they were even thought dangerous to, and subversive of, the existing social order; hence his works were for a long time under censure. Still, the words of this mastermind found permanent lodgment in the heart of the samurai.

---

[14] Devout or zealous worshippers.

[15] Articles of faith.

[16] Deriving from China, Confucianism was introduced into Japan around the fifth century. Although it has religious aspects, Confucianism is generally thought of as a system of philosophical, ethical and political thought. Particularly important in the propagation of Confucianism in Japan from the mid-thirteenth century were two sets of texts: "The Four Books" comprising *The Great Learning, The Doctrine of the Mean, The Analects and Mencius*, and "The Five Classics" consisting of *The Book of Changes, The Book of Documents, The Book of Odes, The Book of Rites* and *The Spring and Autumn Annals*. These texts became mandatory reading for warriors, especially during the Edo period when Confucianism was officially patronized by the shogunate.

[17] Kind, especially to inferiors.

The writings of Confucius and Mencius formed the principal textbooks for youths and the highest authority in discussion among the old. A mere acquaintance with the classics of these two sages was held, however, in no high esteem. A common proverb ridicules one who has only an intellectual knowledge of Confucius, as a man ever studious but ignorant of *Analects*. A typical samurai calls a literary savant a book-smelling sot.[18] Another compares learning to an ill-smelling vegetable that must be boiled and boiled before it is fit for use.[19] A man who has read little smells a little pedantic, and a man who has read much smells yet more so; both are alike unpleasant. The writer meant thereby that knowledge becomes really such only when it is assimilated in the mind of the learner and shows in his character. An intellectual specialist was considered a machine. Intellect itself was considered subordinate to ethical emotion. Man and the universe were conceived to be alike spiritual and ethical. Bushido could not accept the judgment of Huxley, that the cosmic process was unmoral.[20]

Bushido made light of knowledge as such. It was not pursued as an end in itself, but as a means to the attainment of wisdom. Hence,

---

[18] This "typical samurai" is probably a reference to Saigō Takamori (1827–77), a central figure leading to the Meiji Restoration (1868) when the shogunate was replaced with an imperial government. He was also the leader of the rebel army in the Satsuma Rebellion (1877) where he fought against the imperial government he had helped to establish. In 1869, Saigō reprimanded a group of young samurai heading for Kyoto to study Confucian philosophy lest they become "bookworms." Most references to these Confucian scholars are quoted from translations by James Legge (1815–97), *The Chinese Classics: with a Translation, Critical and Exegetical Notes, Prolegomena, and Copious Indexes*, 5 vols. (1861–72). Of particular relevance is vol. 1, *Confucian Analects, the Great Learning, and the Doctrine of the Mean* (1861) and vol. 2, *The Works of Mencius* (1861). These are available in their entirety online.

[19] Miura Baien (1723–89), a physician and Confucian scholar who resided in Bungo (present-day Oita prefecture). This is an odd statement for a scholar to make.

[20] Thomas Henry Huxley (1825–95), an English biologist known as "Darwin's Bulldog" for his support of Charles Darwin's theory of evolution.

he who stopped short of this end was regarded no higher than a convenient machine, which could turn out poems and maxims at bidding. Thus, knowledge was conceived as identical with its practical application in life; and this Socratic doctrine found its greatest exponent in the Chinese philosopher, Wan Yang Ming,[21] who never wearies of repeating, "To know and to act are one and the same." I beg leave for a moment's digression while I am on this subject, inasmuch as some of the noblest types of bushi were strongly influenced by the teachings of this sage. Western readers will easily recognize in his writings many parallels to the New Testament. Making allowance for the terms peculiar to either teaching, the passage, "Seek ye first the kingdom of God and his righteousness; and all these things shall be added unto you,"[22] conveys a thought that may be found on almost any page of Wan Yang Ming. A Japanese disciple[23] of his says—"The lord of heaven and earth, of all living beings, dwelling in the heart of man, becomes his mind (*Kokoro*); hence a mind is a living thing, and is ever luminous" and again, "The spiritual light of our essential being is pure, and is not affected by the will of man. Spontaneously springing up in our mind, it shows what is right and wrong: it is then called conscience; it is even the light that proceedeth from the god of heaven." How very much do these words sound like some passages from Isaac Pennington[24] or other philosophic mystics! I am inclined to think that the Japanese mind, as expressed in the simple tenets of the Shinto religion, was particularly open to the reception of Yang Ming's precepts. He carried his doctrine of the infallibility of conscience to

[21] Wang Yang Ming (1472–1529; J: Ō Yōmei), a Chinese scholar active during the Ming dynasty (1368–1644). He formulated a system of thought that emphasized "good knowledge" (Ch: *liangzhi*; J: *ryōchi*), which was intrinsic in all human beings.

[22] Matthew 6:33.

[23] Miwa Shissai (1669–1744), a Confucian scholar of the Edo period who popularized Wang Yang Ming thought.

[24] Isaac Penington (1616–79), an early member of the Society of Friends (Quakers) in England.

extreme transcendentalism, attributing to it the faculty to perceive, not only the distinction between right and wrong, but also the nature of psychical facts and physical phenomena.[25] He went as far as, if not farther than, Berkeley and Fichte, in Idealism,[26] denying the existence of things outside of human ken.[27] If his system had all the logical errors charged to Solipsism,[28] it had all the efficacy of strong conviction, and its moral import in developing individuality of character and equanimity of temper cannot be gainsaid.[29]

Thus, whatever the sources, the essential principles which Bushido imbibed from them and assimilated to itself, were few and simple. Few and simple as these were, they were sufficient to furnish a safe conduct of life even through the unsafe days of the most unsettled period of our nation's history. The wholesome unsophisticated nature of our warrior ancestors derived ample food for their spirit from a sheaf of commonplace and fragmentary teachings, gleaned as it were on the highways and byways of ancient thought, and, stimulated by the demands of the age, formed from these gleanings a new and unique type of manhood. An acute French savant, M. de la Mazelière,[30] thus sums up his impressions of the sixteenth century: "Toward the middle of the sixteenth century, all is confusion in Japan, in the government, in society, in the church. But the civil wars, the manners returning to barbarism, the necessity for each to execute justice for himself—these formed men comparable to

---

[25] Relating to the human body and soul.

[26] Subjective idealism is a philosophical view based on the idea that nothing exists except through a perceiving mind. Based on the work of Immanuel Kant (1724–1804), the German philosopher Johann Gottlieb Fichte (1762–1814) found the source of his idealism in the "I" or Ego.

[27] An individual's breadth of knowledge or understanding.

[28] Solipsism is the idea that the only thing that truly exists is the mind.

[29] To deny, dispute or contradict.

[30] Marquis de La Mazelière (1864–1937), the author of *Le Japon Histoire et Civilization* (1907–23).

those Italians of the sixteenth century, in whom Taine[31] praises 'the vigorous initiative, the habit of sudden resolutions and desperate undertakings, the grand capacity to do and to suffer.' In Japan as in Italy 'the rude manners of the Middle Ages' made of man a superb animal, 'wholly militant and wholly resistant.' And this is why the sixteenth century displays in the highest degree the principal quality of the Japanese race, that great diversity which one finds there between minds (*esprits*) as well as between temperaments. While in India and even in China men seem to differ chiefly in degree of energy or intelligence, in Japan they differ by originality of character as well. Now, individuality is the sign of superior races and of civilizations already developed. If we make use of an expression dear to Nietzsche,[32] we might say that in Asia, to speak of humanity is to speak of its plains; in Japan as in Europe, one represents it above all by its mountains."

To the pervading characteristics of the men of whom M. de la Mazelière writes, let us now address ourselves. I shall begin with Rectitude.[33]

---

[31] Hippolyte Adolphe Taine (1828–93), a French critic and historian who influenced theories of naturalism, sociological positivism and historicist criticism. He pioneered a contextual approach to studying art based on "race, milieu, and moment."

[32] Friedrich Wilhelm Nietzsche (1844–1900), one of the great German philosophers who influenced the philosophy and modern intellectual history of the West.

[33] Moral integrity or righteousness.

CHAPTER III

Rectitude or Justice

Here we discern the most cogent precept in the code of the samurai. Nothing is more loathsome to him than underhand dealings and crooked undertakings. The conception of Rectitude may be erroneous—it may be narrow. A well-known bushi defines it as a power of resolution—"Rectitude is the power of deciding upon a certain course of conduct in accordance with reason, without wavering—to die when it is right to die, to strike when to strike is right."[1] Another speaks of it in the following terms: "Rectitude is the bone that gives firmness and stature. As without bones the head cannot rest on the top of the spine, nor hands move nor feet stand, so without rectitude neither talent nor learning can make of a human frame a samurai. With it the lack of accomplishments is as nothing."[2] Mencius calls Benevolence man's mind, and Rectitude or Righteousness his path. "How lamentable," he exclaims, "is it to neglect the path and not pursue it, to lose the mind and not know to seek it again! When men's fowls and dogs are lost, they know to seek for them again, but they lose their mind and do not know to seek for it." Have we not here "as in a glass darkly"[3] a

---

[1] Hayashi Shihei (1738–93), a political theorist of the mid-Edo period who advocated creating modern naval and coastal defenses for Japan. The shogunate considered his works seditious and imprisoned him.

[2] Maki Yasuomi (1813–64), a Shinto priest and advocate for imperial restoration during the late Edo period.

[3] Corinthians 13:12. "For now we see through a glass, darkly; but then face to face: now I know in part; but then shall I know even as also I." In other words, "Now we see things imperfectly, like puzzling reflections in a mirror…."

parable propounded three hundred years later in another clime and by a greater Teacher, Who called Himself the Way of righteousness, through whom the lost could be found?[4] But I stray from my point. Righteousness, according to Mencius, is a straight and narrow path which a man ought to take to regain the lost paradise.

Even in the latter days of feudalism,[5] when the long continuance of peace brought leisure into the life of the warrior class, and with it dissipations of all kinds and accomplishments of gentle arts, the epithet *Gishi* (a man of rectitude) was considered superior to any name that signified mastery of learning or art. The Forty-seven Faithfuls—of whom so much is made in our popular education—are known in common parlance as the Forty-seven *Gishi*.[6]

In times when cunning artifice was liable to pass for military tact and downright falsehood for *ruse de guerre*,[7] this manly virtue, frank and honest, was a jewel that shone the brightest and was most highly praised. Rectitude is a twin brother to Valor, another martial virtue. But before proceeding to speak of Valor, let me linger a little while on what I may term a derivation from Rectitude, which, at first deviating slightly from its original, became more and more removed from it, until its meaning was perverted in the popular acceptance. I speak of *Gi-ri*,[8] literally the Right Reason, but which came in time to mean a vague sense of duty which public opinion expects an incumbent to fulfill. In its original and unalloyed sense, it meant duty, pure and simple—hence, we speak of the *Giri* we owe to parents, to superiors, to inferiors, to society at large, and

---

[4] A reference to Jesus Christ.

[5] The Edo period (1603–1868).

[6] The "Revenge of the 47 Rōnin" (masterless *samurai*), a vendetta carried out by Akō warriors in Edo on January 31, 1703 to avenge their master's death is one of the most fêted illustrations of loyalty and warrior ethics in Japanese history.

[7] Ruse of war or military deception.

[8] *Giri* refers to the social and moral obligation of acting appropriately according to the unwritten rules of society viz-a-viz other persons.

so forth. In these instances *Giri* is duty; for what else is duty than what Right Reason demands and commands us to do? Should not Right Reason be our categorical imperative?

Giri primarily meant no more than duty, and I dare say its etymology was derived from the fact, that in our conduct, say to our parents, though love should be the only motive, lacking that, there must be some other authority to enforce filial piety; and they formulated this authority in *Giri*. Very rightly did they formulate this authority—*Giri*—since if love does not rush to deeds of virtue, recourse must be had to man's intellect and his reason must be quickened to convince him of the necessity of acting aright. The same is true of any other moral obligation. The instant Duty becomes onerous; Right Reason steps in to prevent our shirking it. *Giri* thus understood is a severe taskmaster, with a birch-rod in his hand to make sluggards[9] perform their part. It is a secondary power in ethics; as a motive it is infinitely inferior to the Christian doctrine of love, which should be the law. I deem it a product of the conditions of an artificial society—of a society in which accident of birth and unmerited favor instituted class distinctions, in which the family was the social unit, in which seniority of age was of more account than superiority of talents, in which natural affections had often to succumb before arbitrary man-made customs. Because of this very artificiality, *Giri* in time degenerated into a vague sense of propriety called up to explain this and sanction that—as, for example, why a mother must, if need be, sacrifice all her other children in order to save the first-born; or why a daughter must sell her chastity to get funds to pay for the father's dissipation,[10] and the like. Starting as Right Reason, *Giri* has, in my opinion, often stooped to casuistry. It has even degenerated into cowardly fear of censure. I might say of *Giri* what Scott wrote of patriotism, that "as it is the fairest, so

---

[9] Habitually lazy people.

[10] Wasteful expenditure.

it is often the most suspicious, mask of other feelings."[11] Carried beyond or below Right Reason, *Giri* became a monstrous misnomer. It harbored under its wings every sort of sophistry and hypocrisy. It would have been easily turned into a nest of cowardice, if Bushido had not a keen and correct sense of courage, the spirit of daring and bearing.

---

[11] Sir Walter Scott (1771–1832). Quoted from *Waverley* (1814).

CHAPTER IV

Courage, the Spirit of Daring and Bearing

Courage was scarcely deemed worthy to be counted among virtues, unless it was exercised in the cause of Righteousness. In his *Analects* Confucius defines Courage by explaining, as is often his wont, what its negative is. "Perceiving what is right," he says, "and doing it not, argues lack of courage." Put this epigram into a positive statement, and it runs, "Courage is doing what is right." To run all kinds of hazards, to jeopardize one's self, to rush into the jaws of death—these are too often identified with Valor, and in the profession of arms such rashness of conduct—what Shakespeare calls "valor misbegot"[1]—is unjustly applauded; but not so in the Precepts of Knighthood. Death for a cause unworthy of dying for, was called a "dog's death." "To rush into the thick of battle and to be slain in it," says a Prince of Mito,[2] "is easy enough, and the merest churl[3] is equal to the task; but," he continues, "it is true courage to live when it is right to live, and to die only when it is right to die"—and yet the prince had not even heard of the name of Plato, who defines courage as "the knowledge of things that a man should fear and that he should not fear."[4] A distinction which

---

[1] In *Timon of Athens* when the First Senator scolds Alcibiades.

[2] Tokugawa (Mito) Mitsukuni (1628–1700), grandson of Tokugawa Ieyasu and the second *daimyō* of the Mito domain.

[3] A lowly fellow.

[4] Quoted from *Protagoras* by Plato (427–347 BC).

is made in the West between moral and physical courage has long been recognized among us. What samurai youth has not heard of "Great Valor" and the "Valor of a Villain"?

Valor, Fortitude, Bravery, Fearlessness, Courage, being the qualities of soul which appeal most easily to juvenile minds, and which can be trained by exercise and example, were, so to speak, the most popular virtues, early emulated among the youth. Stories of military exploits were repeated almost before boys left their mother's breast. Does a little booby cry for any ache? The mother scolds him in this fashion: "What a coward to cry for a trifling pain! What will you do when your arm is cut off in battle? What when you are called upon to commit *hara-kiri*?"[5] We all know the pathetic fortitude of a famished little boy-prince of Sendai,[6] who in the drama is made to say to his little page, "Seest thou those tiny sparrows in the nest, how their yellow bills are opened wide, and now see! There comes their mother with worms to feed them. How eagerly and happily the little ones eat! But for a samurai, when his stomach is empty, it is a disgrace to feel hungry." Anecdotes of fortitude and bravery abound in nursery tales, though stories of this kind are not by any means the only method of early imbuing the spirit with daring and fearlessness. Parents, with sternness sometimes verging on cruelty, set their children to tasks that called forth all the pluck that was in them. "Bears hurl their cubs down the gorge," they said.[7] Samurai's sons were let down to steep valleys of hard-

---

[5] Ritual disembowelment. Properly known as *seppuku*.

[6] A reference to the character Tsuruchiyo in the 1777 Kabuki play "Meiboku Sendai Hagi" about a succession squabble in the Date clan. Masaoka, the wet nurse, sacrifices her own son to safeguard the young lord Tsuruchiyo, boy-prince of Sendai.

[7] Although Nitobe writes "bear," he is alluding to a Shishi, a mythological beast resembling a lion. It was believed that a Shishi would test its cubs by first throwing them into an abyss, and only if the cubs could claw back by themselves would the Shishi look after them.

ship, and spurred to Sisyphus-like tasks.[8] Occasional deprivation of food or exposure to cold was considered a highly efficacious test for inuring them to endurance. Children of tender age were sent among utter strangers with some message to deliver, were made to rise before the sun, and before breakfast attend to their reading exercises, walking to their teachers with bare feet in the cold of winter; they frequently—once or twice a month, as on the festival of a god of learning[9]—came together in small groups and passed the night without sleep, in reading aloud by turns. Pilgrimages to all sorts of uncanny places—to execution grounds, to graveyards, to houses reputed of being haunted, were favorite pastimes of the young. In the days when decapitation was public, not only were small boys sent to witness the ghastly scene, but they were made to visit alone the place in the darkness of night and there to leave a mark of their visit on the trunkless head.

Does this ultra-Spartan system[10] of "drilling the nerves" strike

---

[8] Futile or pointless. In Greek mythology, Sisyphus was the king of Ephyra (Corinth). To punish him for his arrogance and deceit, he was made to eternally roll a giant boulder up a hill, only to have it roll down and hit him.

[9] Sugawara-no-Michizane (845–903), an aristocrat and scholar who was sent into exile. When disasters befell Kyoto following his death, it was attributed to his angry spirit, and he was enshrined in the Kitano Tenmangū Shrine to placate the "angry ghost." He is still regarded as the deity of study and learning.

[10] [The spiritual aspect of valor is evidenced by composure—calm presence of mind. Tranquility is courage in repose. It is a statical manifestation of valor, as daring deeds are a dynamical. A truly brave man is ever serene; he is never taken by surprise; nothing ruffles the equanimity of his spirit. In the heat of battle he remains cool; in the midst of catastrophes he keeps level his mind. Earthquakes do not shake him, he laughs at storms. We admire him as truly great, who, in the menacing presence of danger or death, retains his self-possession; who, for instance, can compose a poem under impending peril, or hum a strain in the face of death. Such indulgence betraying no tremor in the writing or in the voice is taken as an infallible index of a large nature—of what we call a capacious mind (yoyu), which, far from being pressed or crowded, has always room for something more.

It passes current among us as a piece of authentic history, that as Ota Dokan, the great builder of the castle of Tokyo, was pierced through with a spear, his assassin, knowing the poetical predilection of his victim, accompanied his thrust with this couplet:

> Ah! how in moments like these
> Our heart doth grudge the light of life;

whereupon the expiring hero, not one whit daunted by the mortal wound in his side, added the lines:

> Had not in hours of peace,
> It learned to lightly look on life.

There is even a sportive element in a courageous nature. Things which are serious to ordinary people may be but play to the valiant. Hence in old warfare it was not at all rare for the parties to a conflict to exchange repartee or to begin a rhetorical contest. Combat was not solely a matter of brute force; it was, as well, an intellectual engagement.

Of such character was the battle fought on the banks of the Koromo River, late in the eleventh century. The eastern army routed, its leader, Sadato, took to flight. When the pursuing general pressed him hard and called aloud, "It is a disgrace for a warrior to show his back to the enemy," Sadato reined his horse; upon this the conquering chief shouted an impromptu verse:

> Torn into shreds is the warp of the cloth (*koromo*).

Scarcely had the words escaped his lips when the defeated warrior, undismayed, completed the couplet:

> Since age has worn its threads by use.

Yoshiie, whose bow had all the while been bent, suddenly unstrung it and turned away, leaving his prospective victim to do as he pleased. When asked the reason of his strange behavior, he replied that he could not bear to put to shame one who had kept his presence of mind while hotly pursued by his enemy.

The sorrow which overtook Antony and Octavius at the death of Brutus has been the general experience of brave men. Kenshin, who fought for fourteen years with Shingen, when he heard of the latter's death, wept aloud at the loss of "the best of enemies." It was this same Kenshin who had set a noble example for all time in his treatment of Shingen, whose provinces lay in a mountainous region quite away from the sea, and who had consequently depended upon the Hōjō provinces of the Tōkaidō for salt. The Hōjō prince wishing to weaken him, although not openly at war with him, had cut off from Shingen all traffic in this important article. Kenshin, hearing of his enemy's dilemma and able to obtain his salt from the coast of his own dominions, wrote Shingen that in his opinion the Hōjō lord had committed a very mean act, and that although he (Kenshin) was at war with him (Shingen) he had ordered his subjects to furnish him with

the modern pedagogist[11] with horror and doubt—doubt whether the tendency would not be brutalizing, nipping in the bud the tender emotions of the heart? Let us see in another chapter what other concepts Bushido had of Valor.

---

plenty of salt—adding, "I do not fight with salt, but with the sword," affording more than a parallel to the words of Camillus, "We Romans do not fight with gold, but with iron." Nietzsche spoke for the Samurai heart when he wrote, "You are to be proud of your enemy; then the success of your enemy is your success also." Indeed, valor and honor alike required that we should own as enemies in war only such as prove worthy of being friends in peace. When valor attains this height, it becomes akin to Benevolence.]

[11] Teacher.

CHAPTER V

Benevolence, the Feeling of Distress

L ove, magnanimity, affection for others, sympathy, and pity, were ever recognized to be supreme virtues, the highest of all the attributes of the human soul. It was deemed a princely virtue in a twofold sense: princely among the manifold attributes of a noble spirit; princely as particularly befitting a princely profession. We needed no Shakespeare to feel—though, perhaps, like the rest of the world, we needed him to express it—that mercy became a monarch better than his crown, that it was above his sceptered sway. How often both Confucius and Mencius repeat the highest requirement of a ruler of men to consist in benevolence. Confucius would say—"Let but a prince cultivate virtue, people will flock to him; with people will come to him lands; lands will bring forth for him wealth; wealth will give him the benefit of right uses. Virtue is the root, and wealth an outcome." Again, "Never has there been a case of a sovereign loving benevolence, and the people not loving righteousness."[1] Mencius follows close at his heels and says, "Instances are on record where individuals attained to supreme power in a single state, without benevolence, but never have I heard of a whole empire falling into the hands of one who lacked this virtue."[2]

---

[1] The quotes are from the classic Confucian text, the *Great Learning*, Chapter 10:6–7, 21.

[2] Legge (trans.), *The Works of Mencius* (hereafter referred to as *Mencius*), 7B:13.

Also—it is impossible that any one should become ruler of the people to whom they have not yielded the subjection of their hearts. Both defined this indispensable requirement in a ruler by saying, "Benevolence—benevolence is Man."[3]

Under the regime of feudalism, which could easily degenerate into militarism, it was to benevolence that we owed our deliverance from despotism of the worst kind. An utter surrender of "life and limb" on the part of the governed would have left nothing for the governing but self-will, and this has for its natural consequence the growth of that absolutism[4] so often called "oriental despotism," as though there were no despots of occidental history![5]

Let it be far from me to uphold despotism of any sort; but it is a mistake to identify feudalism with it. When Frederick the Great wrote that "Kings are the first servants of the State,"[6] jurists thought rightly that a new era was reached in the development of freedom. Strangely coinciding in time, in the backwoods of northwestern Japan, Yozan of Yonézawa[7] made exactly the same declaration, showing that feudalism was not all tyranny and oppression. A feudal prince, although unmindful of owing reciprocal obligations to his vassals, felt a higher sense of responsibility to his ancestors and to Heaven. He was a father to his subjects, whom Heaven entrusted to his care. According to the ancient Chinese *Book of Poetry*, "Until the house of Yin lost the hearts of the people, they could appear before Heaven."[8] And Confucius in his *Great Learning* taught: "When

---

[3] *Doctrine of the Mean*, Chapter 20:5. *Mencius*, 7B:16.

[4] The principle or the exercise of complete and unrestricted power in government.

[5] Despotic government historically thought to be characteristic of the Ottoman and Chinese empires.

[6] Frederick II (1712–86), King of Prussia and one of the so-called "enlightened despots" of eighteenth-century Europe. In *Political Testament* (1752).

[7] Uesugi Yōzan (1751–1822), reformist tenth *daimyō* of the Yonezawa domain (now part of Yamagata prefecture).

[8] The earliest compilation of Chinese poems, the *Book of Poetry* was allegedly edited by Confucius.

the prince loves what the people love and hates what the people hate, then is he what is called the parent of the people."[9] Thus are public opinion and monarchical will or democracy and absolutism merged one in the other. Thus also, in a sense not usually assigned to the term, Bushido accepted and corroborated paternal government—paternal also as opposed to the less interested avuncular[10] government. (Uncle Sam's, to wit!)[11] The difference between a despotic and a paternal government lies in this, that in the one the people obey reluctantly, while in the other they do so with "that proud submission, that dignified obedience, that subordination of heart which kept alive, even in servitude itself, the spirit of exalted freedom."[12] The old saying is not entirely false which called the king of England the "king of devils, because of his subjects' often insurrections against, and depositions of, their princes," and which made the French monarch the "king of asses," because of infinite taxes and impositions, but which gave the title of the king of men to the sovereign of Spain "because of his subjects' willing obedience."[13] But enough!

Virtue and absolute power may strike the Anglo-Saxon mind as terms which it is impossible to harmonize. Pobedonostsev[14] has clearly set forth before us the contrast in the foundations of English and other European communities; namely, that these were organized on the basis of common interest, while that was distinguished by a strongly developed independent personality. What this Russian statesman says of the personal dependence of individuals on some social alliance and in the end of ends on the State,

---

[9] *Great Learning*, Chapter 10:3.

[10] Kind or friendly towards inferiors.

[11] Namely, the United States.

[12] [Edmund Burke, *Reflections on the French Revolution* (1790).]

[13] Quoted from monarchist Robert Filmer's (1588–1653) *Patriarcha* (1680).

[14] Konstantin Petrovich Pobedonostsev (1827–1907), a Russian statesman and high-ranking adviser to three successive Tsars.

among the continental nations of Europe and particularly among Slavonic peoples, is doubly true of the Japanese. Hence not only is a free exercise of monarchical power not felt as heavily by us as in Europe, but it is generally moderated by paternal consideration for the feelings of the people. "Absolutism," says Bismarck, "primarily demands in the ruler impartiality, honesty, devotion to duty, energy and inward humility."[15] If I may be allowed to make one more quotation on this subject, I will cite from the speech of the German Emperor at Koblenz,[16] in which he spoke of "Kingship, by the grace of God, with its heavy duties, its tremendous responsibilities to the Creator alone, from which no man, no minister, no parliament, can release the monarch."

We knew benevolence was a tender virtue and mother-like. If upright Rectitude and stern Justice were peculiarly masculine, Mercy had the gentleness and the persuasiveness of a feminine nature. We were warned against indulging in indiscriminate charity, without seasoning it with justice and rectitude. Masamuné[17] expressed it well in his oft-quoted aphorism—"Rectitude carried to excess hardens into stiffness; benevolence indulged beyond measure sinks into weakness."

Fortunately mercy was not so rare as it was beautiful, for it is universally true that "The bravest are the tenderest, the loving are the daring."[18] "*Bushi no nasaké*"—the tenderness of a warrior—

---

[15] Otto Eduard Leopold, Prince of Bismarck (1815–98), also known as Otto von Bismarck, one of the central figures in the formation of the modern German state. Nitobe is quoting from his memoirs, *Bismarck: The Man and the Statesman* (1889).

[16] Emperor Wilhelm I (1797–1888). On becoming the King of Prussia in 1861, he appointed Bismarck as his Minister President. When they successfully unified Germany, Wilhelm became the first emperor. He had formerly lived in Koblenz as the military governor for the Rhine province.

[17] Date Masamune (1567–1636), lord of Yonezawa domain in what is now Yamagata prefecture.

[18] Cited from "The Song of the Camp," an 1863 poem by the Quaker Bayard Tay-

had a sound which appealed at once to whatever was noble in us; not that the mercy of a samurai was generically different from the mercy of any other being, but because it implied mercy where mercy was not a blind impulse, but where it recognized due regard to justice, and where mercy did not remain merely a certain state of mind, but where it was backed with power to save or kill. As economists speak of demand as being effectual or ineffectual, similarly we may call the mercy of bushi effectual, since it implied the power of acting for the good or detriment of the recipient.

Priding themselves as they did in their brute strength and privileges to turn it into account, the samurai gave full consent to what Mencius taught concerning the power of love. "Benevolence,"[19] he says, "brings under its sway whatever hinders its power, just as water subdues fire: they only doubt the power of water to quench flames who try to extinguish with a cupful a whole burning wagon-load of fagots."[20] He also says that "the feeling of distress is the root of benevolence," therefore a benevolent man is ever mindful of those who are suffering and in distress. Thus did Mencius long anticipate Adam Smith who founds his ethical philosophy on sympathy.[21]

It is indeed striking how closely the code of knightly honor of one country coincides with that of others; in other words, how the much-abused oriental ideas of morals find their counterparts in the noblest maxims of European literature. If the well-known lines,

Hae tibi erunt artes—pacisque imponere morem,
Parcere subjectis, et debellare superbos,[22]

---

lor (1825–78), who accompanied Commodore Matthew Perry to Japan in 1853.

[19] *Mencius*, 6A:18.

[20] A bundle of sticks for firewood.

[21] Adam Smith (1723–90), a Scottish economist and philosopher active in the Scottish Enlightenment era.

[22] "These shall be your arts, to set forth the law of peace, to spare the conquered, and to subdue the proud."

were shown a Japanese gentleman, he might readily accuse the Man-
tuan bard of plagiarizing from the literature of his own country.[23]

Benevolence to the weak, the downtrodden or the vanquished
was ever extolled as peculiarly becoming to a samurai. Lovers of
Japanese art must be familiar with the representation of a priest
riding backwards on a cow. The rider was once a warrior who in
his day made his name a byword of terror. In that terrible battle of
Sumano-ura (1184 A.D.),[24] which was one of the most decisive in
our history, he overtook an enemy and in single combat had him in
the clutch of his gigantic arms.[25] Now the etiquette of war required
that on such occasions no blood should be spilt, unless the weaker
party proved to be a man of rank or ability equal to that of the stronger. The grim combatant would have the name of the man under
him; but he refusing to make it known, his helmet was ruthlessly
torn off, when the sight of a juvenile face, fair and beardless, made
the astonished knight relax his hold. Helping the youth to his feet,
in paternal tones he bade the stripling go: "Off, young prince, to thy
mother's side! The sword of Kumagayé[26] shall never be tarnished by
a drop of thy blood. Haste and flee o'er yon pass before thine enemies
come in sight!" The young warrior refused to go and begged Kumagayé, for the honor of both, to dispatch him on the spot. Above
the hoary[27] head of the veteran gleams the cold blade, which many

---

[23] The citation is from *Aeneid* by Publius Vergilius Maro (70–19 BC). Usually
called Virgil, he is widely lauded as one of Ancient Rome's greatest poets. He
was born near Mantua in Cisalpine Gaul.

[24] The Battle of Ichi-no-Tani where the Taira clan lost a decisive confrontation to
Minamoto during the Gempei War (1180–85).

[25] Kumagai-no-Jirō Naozane (1141–1208, a celebrated warrior who served the
Minamoto clan. The tale outlined here of him reluctantly slaying the young
Taira-no-Astumori at the Battle of Ichi-no-Tani is considered a representative
tragic tale of the Gempei War.

[26] His family name was Kumagai, but in popular culture he has long been referred
to as Kumagae.

[27] Gray or white with age.

a time before has sundered the chords of life, but his stout heart quails; there flashes athwart[28] his mental eye the vision of his own boy, who this selfsame day marched to the sound of a bugle to try his maiden arms; the strong hand of the warrior quivers; again he begs his victim to flee for his life. Finding all his entreaties vain and hearing the approaching steps of his comrades, he exclaims: "If thou art overtaken, thou mayst fall at a more ignoble hand than mine. O thou Infinite! receive his soul!" In an instant the sword flashes in the air, and when it falls, it is red with adolescent blood. When the war is ended, we find our soldier returning in triumph, but little cares he now for honor or fame; he renounces his warlike career, shaves his head, dons a priestly garb, devotes the rest of his days to holy pilgrimage, never turning his back to the West where lies the Paradise whence salvation comes and whither the sun hastes daily for his rest.

Critics may point out flaws in this story, which is casuistically vulnerable. Let it be: all the same it shows that Tenderness, Pity, and Love were traits which adorned the most sanguinary[29] exploits of a samurai. It was an old maxim among them that "It becometh not the fowler to slay the bird which takes refuge in his bosom."[30] This in a large measure explains why the Red Cross movement, considered so peculiarly Christian, so readily found a firm footing among us.[31] Decades before we heard of the Geneva Convention, Bakin,[32] our greatest novelist, had familiarized us with the medical treat-

---

[28] From side to side or crosswise.

[29] Attended by bloodshed.

[30] Found in the "Family Instructions of the Yan Clan" (*Ganshi kakun* in Japanese), compiled by Yan Zhitui (531–91).

[31] The Hakuaisha was a society established in 1877 to treat battle casualties in the Satsuma Rebellion. It was affiliated with the International Committee of the Red Cross in 1887 and became the Japanese Red Cross Society.

[32] Takizawa (or Kyokuei) Bakin (1767–1848), a scholar and novelist whose most famous historical romance was *Nansō Satomi Hakken-den* (The Eight Dog Chronicles), 1814–42.

ment of a fallen foe. In the principality of Satsuma,[33] noted for its martial spirit and education, the custom prevailed for young men to practice music; not the blast of trumpets or the beat of drums— "those clamorous harbingers of blood and death"[34]—stirring us to imitate the actions of a tiger, but sad and tender melodies on the *biwa*,[35] soothing our fiery spirits, drawing our thoughts away from scent of blood and scenes of carnage. Polybius[36] tells us of the Constitution of Arcadia, which required all youths under thirty to practice music, in order that this gentle art might alleviate the rigors of the inclement region. It is to its influence that he attributes the absence of cruelty in that part of the Arcadian mountains.

Nor was Satsuma the only place in Japan where gentleness was inculcated among the warrior class. A Prince of Shirakawa[37] jots down his random thoughts, and among them is the following: "Though they come stealing to your bedside in the silent watches of the night, drive not away, but rather cherish these—the fragrance of flowers, the sound of distant bells, the insect hummings of a frosty night." And again, "Though they may wound your feelings, these three you have only to forgive, the breeze that scatters your flowers, the cloud that hides your moon, and the man who tries to pick quarrels with you."

It was ostensibly to express, but actually to cultivate, these gentler emotions that the writing of verses was encouraged. Our poetry has therefore a strong undercurrent of pathos and tenderness. A well-known anecdote of a rustic samurai illustrates the case in

---

[33] Now Kagoshima prefecture.

[34] "Make all our trumpets speak; give them all breath, Those clamorous harbingers of blood and death," *Macbeth*.

[35] [A musical instrument resembling the guitar.]

[36] Polybius (c. 200–c. 118 BC), a Greek-born Roman historian who authored *The Histories*, a detailed work covering the period 264–146 BC.

[37] Matsudaira Sadanobu (1758–1829), *daimyō* of the Shirakawa domain (Fukushima prefecture) and controversial Senior Councilor to the shogunate.

point.[38] When he was told to learn versification, and "The Warbler's Notes"[39] was given him for the subject of his first attempt, his fiery spirit rebelled, and he flung at the feet of his master this uncouth production, which ran

> The brave warrior keeps apart
> The ear that might listen
> To the warbler's song.

His master,[40] undaunted by the crude sentiment, continued to encourage the youth, until one day the music of his soul was awakened to respond to the sweet notes of the *uguisu*, and he wrote

> Stands the warrior, mailed and strong,
> To hear the uguisu's song,
> Warbled sweet the trees among.

We admire and enjoy the heroic incident in Körner's short life, when, as he lay wounded on the battlefield, he scribbled his famous *Farewell to Life*.[41] Incidents of a similar kind were not at all unusual in our warfare. Our pithy, epigrammatic poems[42] were particularly

---

[38] The samurai in question here is Ōwashi Bungo, a character in the popular puppet and Kabuki play "The Treasury of Loyal Retainers" (*Chūshingura*). The story is about the 47 loyal *rōnin* (masterless samurai) in which the character is based on Ōtaka Gengo (1672–1703). Ōtaka took up poetry to divert the attention of authorities who suspected the 47 samurai were plotting unsanctioned revenge in the name of their dead master.

[39] [The *uguisu* or warbler, sometimes called the nightingale of Japan.]

[40] Ōboshi Yuranosuke, leader of the masterless samurai in *Chūshingura* based on Ōishi Kuranosuke (1659–1703).

[41] Carl Theodor Körner (1791–1813), a German poet and soldier in the German Campaign of 1813 against Napoleon. Among his many patriotic verses, he penned "Farewell to Life" when he was injured in battle in June 1813. He was killed two months later.

[42] Witty and succinctly expressed.

well suited to the improvisation of a single sentiment. Everybody of any education was either a poet or a poetaster.[43] Not infrequently a marching soldier might be seen to halt, take his writing utensils from his belt, and compose an ode—and such papers were found afterward in the helmets or the breastplates when these were removed from their lifeless wearers.

What Christianity has done in Europe toward rousing compassion in the midst of belligerent horrors, love of music and letters has done in Japan. The cultivation of tender feelings breeds considerate regard for the sufferings of others. Modesty and complaisance,[44] actuated by respect for others' feelings, are at the root of politeness.

---

[43] A derogatory term applied to bad or inferior poets.
[44] A disposition to please.

CHAPTER VI

Politeness

Courtesy and urbanity of manners have been noticed by every foreign tourist as a marked Japanese trait. Politeness is a poor virtue, if it is actuated only by a fear of offending good taste, whereas it should be the outward manifestation of a sympathetic regard for the feelings of others. It also implies a due regard for the fitness of things, therefore due respect to social positions; for these latter express no plutocratic[1] distinctions, but were originally distinctions for actual merit.

In its highest form, politeness almost approaches love. We may reverently say, politeness "suffereth long, and is kind; envieth not, vaunteth not itself, is not puffed up; doth not behave itself unseemly, seeketh not her own, is not easily provoked, taketh not account of evil."[2] Is it any wonder that Professor Dean,[3] in speaking of the six elements of humanity, accords to politeness an exalted position, inasmuch as it is the ripest fruit of social intercourse?

While thus extolling politeness, far be it from me to put it in the front rank of virtues. If we analyze it, we shall find it correlated with other virtues of a higher order; for what virtue stands alone? While—or rather because—it was exalted as peculiar to the pro-

---

[1] Controlling class of the wealthy.

[2] Corinthians 13:4–5. This is an explanation of the meaning of love.

[3] Amos Dean (1803–68), first president of the University of Iowa and author of the seven-volume *History of Civilization* (1868–69) in which he refers to industry, religion, government, society, philosophy and art as the six elements of humanity. "Politeness," he argues, "is essential in society.

fession of arms, and as such esteemed in a degree higher than its deserts, there came into existence its counterfeits. Confucius himself has repeatedly taught that external appurtenances are as little a part of propriety as sounds are of music.[4]

When propriety was elevated to the *sine qua non*[5] of social intercourse, it was only to be expected that an elaborate system of etiquette should come into vogue to train youth in correct social behavior. How one must bow in accosting others, how he must walk and sit, were taught and learned with utmost care. Table manners grew to be a science. Tea serving and drinking were raised to ceremony. A man of education is, of course, expected to be master of all these. Very fitly does Mr. Veblen, in his interesting book call decorum "a product and an exponent of the leisure-class life."[6]

I have heard slighting remarks made by Europeans upon our elaborate discipline of politeness. It has been criticized as absorbing too much of our thought and in so far a folly to observe strict obedience to it. I admit that there may be unnecessary niceties in ceremonious etiquette, but whether it partakes as much of folly as the adherence to ever-changing fashions of the West, is a question not very clear to my mind. Even fashions I do not consider solely as freaks of vanity; on the contrary, I look upon these as a ceaseless search of the human mind for the beautiful. Much less do I consider elaborate ceremony as altogether trivial; for it denotes the result of long observation as to the most appropriate method of achieving a certain result. If there is anything to do, there is certainly a best way to do it, and the best way is both the most economical and the

---

[4] *Analects*, 17.11. "It is not the external appurtenances which constitute propriety, nor the sound of instruments which constitute music."

[5] An essential action, condition or ingredient.

[6] [*Theory of the Leisure Class* (1899), p. 46.] Thorstein Bunde Veblen (1857–1929) was an American economist who authored *The Theory of the Leisure Class: An Economic Study of Institutions* (1899).

most graceful. Mr. Spencer[7] defines grace as the most economical manner of motion. The tea ceremony presents certain definite
ways of manipulating a bowl, a spoon, a napkin, etc. To a novice
it looks tedious. But one soon discovers that the way prescribed
is, after all, the most saving of time and labor; in other words, the
most economical use of force—hence, according to Spencer's dictum, the most graceful.

The spiritual significance of social decorum—or, I might say,
to borrow from the vocabulary of the "Philosophy of Clothes,"[8]
the spiritual discipline of which etiquette and ceremony are mere
outward garments—is out of all proportion to what their appearance warrants us in believing. I might follow the example of Mr.
Spencer and trace in our ceremonial institutions their origins and
the moral motives that gave rise to them; but that is not what I
shall endeavor to do in this book. It is the moral training involved
in strict observance of propriety, that I wish to emphasize. I have
said that etiquette was elaborated into the finest niceties, so much
so that different schools, advocating different systems, came into
existence. But they all united in the ultimate essential, and this was
put by a great exponent of the best known school of etiquette, the
Ogasawara,[9] in the following terms: "The end of all etiquette is to so
cultivate your mind that even when you are quietly seated, not the

---

[7] Herbert Spencer (1820–1903), a British philosopher, biologist, sociologist and
political theorist who advocated Darwinian theories in his studies of society. It
was Spencer who coined the term "survival of the fittest."

[8] A reference to one of Nitobe's favorite books, Thomas Carlyle's *Sartor Resartus*
(1833–34). See my introduction.

[9] The Ogasawara clan were leaders in devising protocols of etiquette for the samurai class since the rise of warrior hegemony in the twelfth century. Their school
originally centered on skills in archery and horsemanship, but they eventually
formulated rules for daily deportment in the samurai community. The Ogasawara family were also instrumental in the development of national etiquette
standards for schools when Japan was modernizing in the latter half of the nineteenth century. The tradition still exists today.

roughest ruffian can dare make onset on your person."[10] It means, in other words, that by constant exercise in correct manners, one brings all the parts and faculties of his body into perfect order and into such harmony with itself and its environment as to express the mastery of spirit over the flesh. What a new and deep significance the French word *bienséance*[11] comes to contain.

If the promise is true that gracefulness means economy of force, then it follows as a logical sequence that a constant practice of graceful deportment must bring with it a reserve and storage of force. Fine manners, therefore, mean power in repose. When the barbarian Gauls, during the sack of Rome, burst into the assembled Senate and dared pull the beards of the venerable Fathers, we think the old gentlemen were to blame, inasmuch as they lacked dignity and strength of manners.[12] Is lofty spiritual attainment really possible through etiquette? Why not?—All roads lead to Rome!

As an example of how the simplest thing can be made into an art and then become spiritual culture, I may take *Cha-no-yu*, the tea ceremony. Tea-sipping as a fine art! Why should it not be? In the children drawing pictures on the sand, or in the savage carving on a rock, was the promise of a Raphael[13] or a Michelangelo.[14] How much more is the drinking of a beverage, which began with the transcendental contemplation of a Hindu anchorite,[15] entitled to develop into a handmaid of Religion and Morality? That calmness

---

[10] Thought to be the words of Ogasawara Kiyokane (1846–1913), the 28th patriarch of the Ogasawara School.

[11] [Etymologically, well-seatedness.]

[12] 390 BC under Brennus.

[13] Raffaello Sanzio da Urbino (1483–1520), a prominent Italian Renaissance painter and architect.

[14] Michelangelo di Lodovico Buonarroti Simoni (1475–1564), an Italian sculptor and painter of the Renaissance period.

[15] Bodhidharma (?–ca. 530), an Indian monk who established Chan (Zen) Buddhism in China. In Japan, he is known as Daruma. "Anchorite" means somebody who retires from secular society.

of mind, that serenity of temper, that composure and quietness of demeanor which are the first essentials of *Cha-no-yu*, are without doubt the first conditions of right thinking and right feeling. The scrupulous cleanliness of the little room, shut off from sight and sound of the madding crowd, is in itself conducive to direct one's thoughts from the world. The bare interior does not engross one's attention like the innumerable pictures and bric-a-brac of a Western parlor; the presence of *kakémono*[16] calls our attention more to grace of design than to beauty of color. The utmost refinement of taste is the object aimed at; whereas anything like display is banished with religious horror. The very fact that it was invented by a contemplative recluse,[17] in a time when wars and the rumors of wars were incessant, is well calculated to show that this institution was more than a pastime. Before entering the quiet precincts of the tearoom, the company assembling to partake of the ceremony laid aside, together with their swords, the ferocity of battlefield or the cares of government, there to find peace and friendship.

Cha-no-yu is more than a ceremony—it is a fine art;[18] it is poetry, with articulate gestures for rhythms: it is a *modus operandi* of soul discipline. Its greatest value lies in this last phase. Not infrequently the other phases preponderated[19] in the mind of its votaries. But that does not prove that its essence was not of a spiritual

---

[16] [Hanging scrolls, which may be either paintings or ideograms, used for decorative purposes.]

[17] Sen-no-Rikyū (1522–91), a preeminent *cha-no-yu* master who founded the Sen style of tea ceremony. He was the teacher of Toyotomi Hideyoshi, who ordered him for unknown reasons to commit *seppuku*.

[18] It is interesting to note here that one of Nitobe's contemporaries, Okakura Tenshin (aka Kakuzō) (1862–1913), a well-known art critic and philosopher, published several books in English explaining the ideals of Japanese tea and other art forms. These include *The Ideals of the East* (1903), *The Awakening of Japan* (1904) and *The Book of Tea* (1906). Like Nitobe, Okakura started studying English when he was nine, entered the same Tokyo School of Foreign Languages at eleven and then Tokyo Imperial University at fifteen.

[19] To exceed in influence, power or importance.

nature. Politeness will be a great acquisition, if it does no more than impart grace to manners; but its function does not stop here. For propriety, springing as it does from motives of benevolence and modesty, and actuated by tender feelings toward the sensibilities of others, is ever a graceful expression of sympathy. Its requirement is that we should weep with those that weep and rejoice with those that rejoice. Such didactic[20] requirement, when reduced into small everyday details of life, expresses itself in little acts scarcely noticeable, or, if noticed, is, as one missionary lady of twenty years' residence once said to me, "awfully funny." You are out in the hot, glaring sun with no shade over you; a Japanese acquaintance passes by; you accost him, and instantly his hat is off—well, that is perfectly natural, but the "awfully funny" performance is that all the while he talks with you his parasol is down and he stands in the glaring sun also. How foolish!—Yes, exactly so, provided the motive were less than this: "You are in the sun; I sympathize with you; I would willingly take you under my parasol if it were large enough, or if we were familiarly acquainted; as I cannot shade you, I will share your discomforts." Little acts of this kind, equally or more amusing, are not mere gestures or conventionalities. They are the "bodying forth"[21] of thoughtful feelings for the comfort of others.

Another "awfully funny" custom is dictated by our canons of Politeness; but many superficial writers on Japan have dismissed it by simply attributing it to the general topsyturvyness of the nation.[22] Every foreigner who has observed it will confess the awkwardness he felt in making proper reply upon the occasion. In America, when you make a gift, you sing its praises to the recipient;

---

[20] Application of teaching and learning.

[21] Embodiment.

[22] Basil Hall Chamberlain (1850–1935) called Japan "the land of topsy-turvydom" in *Things Japanese* (1890). Chamberlain was equally critical of Nitobe when this book was published and slated it unflatteringly in his *Invention of a New Religion*.

in Japan we depreciate or slander it. The underlying idea with you is, "This is a nice gift: if it were not nice I would not dare give it to you; for it will be an insult to give you anything but what is nice." In contrast to this, our logic runs: "You are a nice person, and no gift is nice enough for you. You will not accept anything I can lay at your feet except as a token of my good will; so accept this, not for its intrinsic value, but as a token. It will be an insult to your worth to call the best gift good enough for you." Place the two ideas side by side, and we see that the ultimate idea is one and the same. Neither is "awfully funny." The American speaks of the material which makes the gift; the Japanese speaks of the spirit which prompts the gift. It is perverse reasoning to conclude, because our sense of propriety shows itself in all the smallest ramifications of our deportment, to take the least important of them and uphold it as the type, and pass judgment upon the principle itself. Which is more important, to eat or to observe rules of propriety about eating? A Chinese sage answers, "If you take a case where the eating is all-important, and the observing the rules of propriety is of little importance, and compare them together, why not merely say that the eating is of the more importance?"[23] "Metal is heavier than feathers," but does that saying have reference to a single clasp of metal and a wagonload of feathers? Take a piece of wood a foot thick and raise it above the pinnacle of a temple, none would call it taller than the temple. To the question, "Which is the more important, to tell the truth or to be polite?" The Japanese are said to give an answer diametrically opposite to what the American will say—but I forbear any comment until I come to speak of veracity and sincerity.

---

[23] *Mencius*, 6B:21.

CHAPTER VII

Veracity and Sincerity

Without veracity and sincerity, politeness is a farce and a show. "Propriety carried beyond right bounds," says Masamuné,[1] "becomes a lie." An ancient poet has out-done Polonius[2] in the advice he gives: "To thyself be faithful: if in thy heart thou strayest not from truth, without prayer of thine the Gods will keep thee whole."[3] The apotheosis[4] of Sincerity to which Confucius gives expression in the *Doctrine of the Mean*, attributes to it transcendental powers, almost identifying them with the Divine. "Sincerity is the end and the beginning of all things; without Sincerity there would be nothing."[5] He then dwells with eloquence on its far-reaching and long-enduring nature, its power to produce changes without movement and by its mere presence to accomplish its purpose without effort. From the Chinese ideogram for Sincerity, which is a combination of "Word" and "Perfect,"[6] one is tempted to draw a parallel between it and the Neo-Platonic doctrine of Logos— to such height does the sage soar in his unwonted mystic flight.[7]

---

[1] Date Masamune (1567–1636).

[2] Polonius is King Claudius's Lord Chamberlain in Shakespeare's *Hamlet*.

[3] Sugawara-no-Michizane (845–903).

[4] Glorification of a subject to a divine level.

[5] *Doctrine of the Mean*, 25:2.

[6] 言＋成 ＝ 誠

[7] "Neo-Platonism" refers to unconventional Platonic philosophy from the time of Plotinus (204–270) up to the sixth century. Plato used *Logos* in reference to the spoken and unspoken word, or the word still in the mind. It may also refer to the rational principle that governs all things.

Lying or equivocation[8] was deemed equally cowardly. The bushi held that his high social position demanded a loftier standard of veracity than that of the tradesman and peasant. *Bushi no ichi-gon*—the word of a samurai, or in exact German equivalent, *Ritterwort*—was sufficient guaranty for the truthfulness of an assertion. His word carried such weight with it that promises were generally made and fulfilled without a written pledge, which would have been deemed quite beneath his dignity. Many thrilling anecdotes were told of those who atoned by death for *ni-gon*, a double tongue.[9]

The regard for veracity was so high that, unlike the generality of Christians who persistently violate the plain commands of the Teacher not to swear, the best of samurai looked upon an oath as derogatory to their honor. I am well aware that they did swear by different deities or upon their swords, but never has swearing degenerated into wanton form and irreverent interjection.[10] To emphasize our words a practice was sometimes resorted to of literally sealing with blood.[11] For the explanation of such a practice, I need only refer my readers to Goethe's *Faust*.[12]

A recent American writer is responsible for this statement, that if you ask an ordinary Japanese which is better, to tell a falsehood or be impolite, he will not hesitate to answer, "To tell a falsehood!" Dr. Peery[13] is partly right and partly wrong; right in that an ordinary Japanese, even a samurai, may answer in the way ascribed to him,

---

[8] Ambiguous expression in order to mislead.

[9] Going back on one's word.

[10] Disrespectful utterance. Profanity.

[11] The thumb would be cut to extract blood, which was used as a kind of signature or seal in written oaths in a practice known as *keppan*.

[12] Johann Wolfgang von Goethe (1749–1832), a central philosopher of the German Enlightenment. *Faust* was published in two parts in 1808 and 1832. Faust was a successful charlatan who wanted more from life so made a pact with the devil to find happiness.

[13] [Peery, *The Gist of Japan*, p. 86.] Rufus Benton Peery (1868–1934) was a Lu-

but wrong in attributing too much weight to the term he translates
"falsehood." This word (in Japanese, *uso*) is employed to denote
anything which is not a truth (*makoto*) or fact (*honto*). Lowell
tells us that Wordsworth could not distinguish between truth and
fact, and an ordinary Japanese is in this respect as good as Wordsworth.[14] Ask a Japanese, or even an American of any refinement,
to tell you whether he dislikes you or whether he is sick to his stomach, and he will not hesitate long to tell falsehoods and answer, "I
like you much," or, "I am quite well, thank you." To sacrifice truth
merely for the sake of politeness was regarded as an "empty form"
(*kyo-rei*) and "deception by sweet words."

I own I am speaking now of the Bushido idea of veracity: but it
may not be amiss to devote a few words to our commercial integrity, of which I have heard much complaint in foreign books and
journals. A loose business morality has indeed been the worst blot
on our national reputation; but before abusing it or hastily con-
demning the whole race for it, let us calmly study it and we shall
be rewarded with consolation for the future.

Of all the great occupations of life, none was farther removed
from the profession of arms than commerce. The merchant was
placed lowest in the category of vocations—the knight, the tiller of
the soil, the mechanic, the merchant. The samurai derived his in-
come from land and could even indulge, if he had a mind to, in am-
ateur farming; but the counter and abacus were abhorred. We know
the wisdom of this social arrangement. Montesquieu has made it
clear that the debarring of the nobility from mercantile pursuits
was an admirable social policy, in that it prevented wealth from ac-
cumulating in the hands of the powerful.[15] The separation of power

---

theran missionary who resided in Saga prefecture. He wrote *The Gist of Japan:
The Islands, Their People, and Missions* in 1897.

[14] James Russell Lowell (1819–91), an American poet. An essay on William Wordsworth (1770–1850) is found in his book *The English Poets* (1888).

[15] Charles de Montesquieu (1689–1755), a French political philosopher who

and riches kept the distribution of the latter more nearly equable. Professor Dill,[16] the author of *Roman Society in the Last Century of the Western Empire,* has brought afresh to our mind that one cause of the decadence of the Roman Empire, was the permission given to the nobility to engage in trade, and the consequent monopoly of wealth and power by a minority of the senatorial families.

Commerce, therefore, in feudal Japan did not reach that degree of development which it would have attained under freer conditions. The obloquy[17] attached to the calling naturally brought within its pale such as cared little for social repute. "Call one a thief and he will steal." Put a stigma on a calling and its followers adjust their morals to it, for it is natural that "the normal conscience," as Hugh Black says, "rises to the demands made on it, and easily falls to the limit of the standard expected from it."[18] It is unnecessary to add that no business, commercial or otherwise, can be transacted without a code of morals. Our merchants of the feudal period had one among themselves, without which they could never have developed, as they did in embryo, such fundamental mercantile institutions as the guild, the bank, the bourse, insurance, checks, bills of exchange, etc.; but in their relations with people outside their vocation, the tradesmen lived too true to the reputation of their order.

This being the case, when the country was opened to foreign trade, only the most adventurous and unscrupulous rushed to the ports, while the respectable business houses declined for some time the repeated requests of the authorities to establish branch houses. Was Bushido powerless to stay the current of commercial

---

championed the segregation of governmental power. Nitobe is referring to his work *De l'esprit des lois* (1748).

[16] Samuel Dill (1844–1924), an Irish scholar who authored *Roman Society in the Last Century of the Western Empire* in 1898.

[17] Abusive language aimed at a person or thing. Negative image

[18] Hugh Black (1868–1953), an American theologian. Nitobe is citing Chapter 11 ("The Medieval Concept of Sainthood") of *Culture and Restraint* (1901).

dishonor? Let us see.

Those who are well acquainted with our history will remember that only a few years after our treaty ports were opened to foreign trade, feudalism was abolished, and when with it the samurai's fiefs were taken and bonds[19] issued to them in compensation, they were given liberty to invest them in mercantile transactions. Now you may ask, "Why could they not bring their much boasted veracity into their new business relations and so reform the old abuses?" Those who had eyes to see could not weep enough; those who had hearts to feel could not sympathize enough, with the fate of many a noble and honest samurai who signally and irrevocably failed in his new and unfamiliar field of trade and industry, through sheer lack of shrewdness in coping with his artful plebeian rival. When we know that 80 percent of the business houses fail in so industrial a country as America, is it any wonder that scarcely one among a hundred samurai who went into trade could succeed in his new vocation? It will be long before it will be recognized how many fortunes were wrecked in the attempt to apply Bushido ethics to business methods; but it was soon patent to every observing mind that the ways of wealth were not the ways of honor. In what respects, then, were they different?

Of the three incentives to veracity that Lecky[20] enumerates, viz., the industrial, the political, and the philosophical, the first was altogether lacking in Bushido. As to the second, it could develop little in a political community under a feudal system. It is in its philosophical and, as Lecky says, in its highest aspect, that honesty at-

---

[19] Public bonds issued were issued to former samurai (*shizoku*) in 1877 to replace hereditary stipends. Having had little previous experience in the world of commerce, many were bankrupted when forced to sell their bonds at a loss. Nitobe's adoptive father used his bonds to establish a clothing shop in Tokyo but it was never successful.

[20] William Edward Hartpole Lecky (1838–1903), an Irish historian. Nitobe is citing vol. I of his *History of European Morals from Augustus to Charlemagne* (1862).

tained elevated rank in our catalogue of virtues. With all my sincere regard for the high commercial integrity of the Anglo-Saxon race, when I ask for the ultimate ground, I am told that "honesty is the best policy"—that it *pays* to be honest. Is not this virtue, then, its own reward? If it is followed because it brings in more cash than falsehood, I am afraid Bushido would rather indulge in lies!

If Bushido rejects a doctrine of *quid pro quo* rewards,[21] the shrewder tradesman will readily accept it. Lecky has very truly remarked that veracity owes its growth largely to commerce and manufacture; as Nietzsche puts it, honesty is the youngest of the virtues—in other words, it is the foster-child of modern industry.[22] Without this mother, veracity was like a blue-blood orphan whom only the most cultivated mind could adopt and nourish. Such minds were general among the samurai, but, for want of a more democratic and utilitarian foster-mother, the tender child failed to thrive. Industries advancing, veracity will prove an easy, nay, a profitable virtue to practice. Just think—as late as November, 1880, Bismarck sent a circular to the professional consuls of the German Empire, warning them of "a lamentable lack of reliability with regard to German shipments *inter alia*,[23] apparent both as to quality and quantity."[24] Nowadays we hear comparatively little of German carelessness and dishonesty in trade. In twenty years her merchants have learned that in the end honesty pays. Already our merchants have found that out. For the rest I recommend the reader to two recent writers for well-weighed judgment on this point.[25] It is inter-

---

[21] An exchange of goods or services.

[22] Friedrich Wilhelm Nietzsche (1844–1900). Nitobe is citing his *Thus Spake Zarathustra* (1885).

[23] Among other things.

[24] Quoted from German historian Heinrich von Poschinger's (1845–1911) *Conversations with Prince Bismarck*.

[25] [Knapp, *Feudal and Modern Japan*, vol. I, ch. iv; Ransome, *Japan in Transition*, ch. viii.] Arthur May Knapp (1841–1921) was a representative of the American Unitarian Association who visited Japan several times from 1887. James Staf-

esting to remark in this connection that integrity and honor were the surest guaranties which even a merchant debtor could present in the form of promissory notes. It was quite a usual thing to insert such clauses as these: "In default of the repayment of the sum lent to me, I shall say nothing against being ridiculed in public"; or, "In case I fail to pay you back, you may call me a fool," and the like.

Often have I wondered whether the veracity of Bushido had any motive higher than courage. In the absence of any positive commandment against bearing false witness, lying was not condemned as sin, but simply denounced as weakness, and, as such, highly dishonorable. As a matter of fact, the idea of honesty is so intimately blended, and its Latin and its German etymology so identified with honor, that it is high time I should pause a few moments for the consideration of this feature of the Precepts of Knighthood.

ford Ransome (1860–1931) was a British journalist and the author of *Japan in Transition: A Comparative Study of the Progress, Policy, and Methods of the Japanese Since Their War with China* (1899).

CHAPTER VIII

Honor

The sense of honor, implying a vivid consciousness of personal dignity and worth, could not fail to characterize the samurai, born and bred to value the duties and privileges of their profession. Though the word ordinarily given nowadays as the translation of honor was not used freely,[1] yet the idea was conveyed by such terms as *na* (name) *men-moku* (countenance), *guai-bun* (outside hearing), reminding us respectively of the biblical use of "name," of the evolution of the term "personality" from the Greek mask, and of "fame." A good name—one's reputation, "the immortal part of one's self, what remains being bestial"[2]—assumed as a matter of course, any infringement upon its integrity was felt as shame, and the sense of shame (*Ren-chi-shin*) was one of the earliest to be cherished in juvenile education. "You will be laughed at," "It will disgrace you," "Are you not ashamed?" were the last appeal to correct behavior on the part of a youthful delinquent. Such a recourse to his honor touched the most sensitive spot in the child's heart, as though it had been nursed on honor while he was in his mother's womb; for most truly is honor a prenatal influence, being closely bound up with strong family consciousness. "In losing the solidarity of families," says Balzac, "society has lost the fundamental force which Montesquieu named Honor."[3]

---

[1] The word *meiyo* (名誉) came into popular usage as a legal term for defamation cases during the Meiji period.

[2] Shakespeare's *Othello*. Cassio's comments to Iago when Othello demoted Cassio.

[3] Honoré de Balzac (1799–1850), a French novelist and playwright. Nitobe is cit-

Indeed, the sense of shame seems to me to be the earliest indication of the moral consciousness of the race. The first and worst punishment which befell humanity in consequence of tasting "the fruit of that forbidden tree"[4] was, to my mind, not the sorrow of childbirth, nor the thorns and thistles, but the awakening of the sense of shame. Few incidents in history excel in pathos the scene of the first mother plying, with heaving breast and tremulous fingers, her crude needle on the few fig leaves which her dejected husband plucked for her.[5] This first fruit of disobedience clings to us with a tenacity that nothing else does. All the sartorial[6] ingenuity of mankind has not yet succeeded in sewing an apron that will efficaciously hide our sense of shame. That samurai was right who refused to compromise his character by a slight humiliation in his youth; "because," he said, "dishonor is like a scar on a tree, which time, instead of effacing, only helps to enlarge."[7]

Mencius had taught centuries before, in almost the identical phrase, what Carlyle has latterly expressed—namely, that "Shame is the soil of all Virtue, of good manners and good morals."[8]

The fear of disgrace was so great that if our literature lacks such eloquence as Shakespeare puts into the mouth of Norfolk,[9] it nevertheless hung like Damocles' sword over the head of every samurai and often assumed a morbid character.[10] In the name of honor,

---

ing *The Village Rector* (1841).

[4] In the Garden of Eden.

[5] Adam and Eve.

[6] Tailored.

[7] Arai Hakuseki (1657–1725), a Confucian scholar who counselled the shogunate.

[8] Another reference to Thomas Carlyle's *Sartor Resartus*, *cited from* Book 3 ("Symbols").

[9] Thomas Mowbray, the Duke of Norfolk in *Richard II*. Mowbray is accused by Henry Bolingbroke of treason and is exiled from England.

[10] The Greek king Dionysius (?431–367 BC) seated Damocles under a sword hanging from the ceiling by a hair above his head to show him how perilous happiness and power are.

deeds were perpetrated which can find no justification in the code of Bushido. At the slightest, nay—imaginary insult—the quick-tempered braggart[11] took offense, resorted to the use of the sword, and many an unnecessary strife was raised and many an innocent life lost.

The story of a well-meaning citizen who called the attention of a bushi to a flea jumping on his back, and who was forthwith cut in two for the simple and questionable reason, that inasmuch as fleas are parasites which feed on animals, it was an unpardonable insult to identify a noble warrior with a beast—I say, stories like these are too frivolous to believe. Yet, the circulation of such stories implies three things: (1) that they were invented to overawe common people; (2) that abuses were really made of the samurai's profession of honor; and (3) that a very strong sense of shame was developed among them. It is plainly unfair to take an abnormal case to cast blame upon the precepts, any more than to judge of the true teachings of Christ from the fruits of religious fanaticism and extravagance— inquisitions and hypocrisy. But, as in religious monomania[12] there is something touchingly noble as compared with the delirium tremens[13] of a drunkard, so in that extreme sensitiveness of the samurai about their honor do we not recognize the substratum of a genuine virtue?

The morbid excess into which the delicate code of honor was inclined to run was strongly counterbalanced by preaching magnanimity and patience. To take offense at slight provocation was ridiculed as "short-tempered." The popular adage said: "To bear what you think you cannot bear is really to bear." The great Iyéyasu[14] left

---

[11] Loud, arrogant boaster.

[12] A psychosis characterized by thoughts confined to one idea or group of ideas. An obsession.

[13] DTs. A severe form of ethanol withdrawal.

[14] Tokugawa Ieyasu (1543–1616), founder of the Tokugawa shogunate (1603–1867) and the third great unifier of Japan after Oda Nobunaga and Toyotomi Hideyoshi.

to posterity a few maxims, among which are the following—"The
life of man is like going a long distance with a heavy load upon the
shoulders. Haste not…. Reproach none, but be forever watchful of
thine own shortcomings…. Forbearance is the basis of length of
days." He proved in his life what he preached. A literary wit[15] put
a characteristic epigram into the mouths of three well-known per-
sonages in our history: to Nobunaga[16] he attributed, "I will kill her,
if the nightingale sings not in time"; to Hidéyoshi, "I will force her
to sing for me"; and to Iyéyasu, "I will wait till she opens her lips."

Patience and long-suffering were also highly commended by
Mencius. In one place he writes to this effect: "Though you de-
nude[17] yourself and insult me, what is that to me? You cannot de-
file my soul by your outrage."[18] Elsewhere he teaches that anger at
a petty offense is unworthy of a superior man, but indignation for
a great cause is righteous wrath.[19]

To what height of unmartial and unresisting meekness Bushido
could reach in some of its votaries, may be seen in their utterances.
Take, for instance, this saying of Ogawa: "When others speak all
manner of evil things against thee, return not evil for evil, but rather reflect that thou wast not more faithful in the discharge of thy
duties."[20] Take another of Kumazawa—"When others blame thee,
blame them not; when others are angry at thee, return not anger.
Joy cometh only as Passion and Desire part."[21] Still another instance

---

[15] A well-known story from Matsura Seizan's (1760–1841) collection of essays.
Saizan was a *daimyō* of the Hirado domain (Nagasaki prefecture), famous for
his skill in swordsmanship.

[16] Oda Nobunaga (1534–82), a ruthless warlord of the Warring States period
credited with being the first of the three unifiers of sixteenth-century Japan,
the other two being Toyotomi Hideyoshi and Tokugawa Ieyasu.

[17] Strip or uncover.

[18] *Mencius*, 2A:9.

[19] *Mencius*, 2B:12.

[20] Ogawa Risshō (1649–96), a Confucian scholar.

[21] Kumagawa Banzan (1619–91), an influential Confucian scholar who ran afoul

I may cite from Saigo,[22] upon whose overhanging brows "Shame is
ashamed to sit"[23]—"The Way is the way of Heaven and Earth; Man's
place is to follow it; therefore make it the object of thy life to reverence Heaven. Heaven loves me and others with equal love; therefore with the love wherewith thou lovest thyself, love others. Make
not Man thy partner but Heaven, and making Heaven thy partner
do thy best. Never condemn others; but see to it that thou comest
not short of thine own mark." Some of these sayings remind us of
Christian expostulations[24] and show us how far in practical morality natural religion can approach the revealed. Not only did these
sayings remain as utterances, but they were really embodied in acts.

It must be admitted that very few attained this sublime height
of magnanimity, patience, and forgiveness. It was a great pity that
nothing clear and general was expressed as to what constitutes
honor, only a few enlightened minds being aware that it "from no
condition rises,"[25] but that it lies in each acting well his part; for
nothing was easier than for youths to forget in the heat of action
what they had learned in Mencius in their calmer moments. Said
this sage: "'Tis in every man's mind to love honor; but little doth
he dream that what is truly honorable lies within himself and not
elsewhere. The honor which men confer is not good honor. Those
whom Châo the Great ennobles, he can make mean again."[26] For
the most part, an insult was quickly resented and repaid by death,
as we shall see later, while honor—too often nothing higher than
vainglory[27] or worldly approbation—was prized as the *summum*

---

of the government when his work was interpreted as being critical of the shogunate.

[22] Saigō Takamori (1827–77). Saigō was renowned for his heavy-set eyebrows.

[23] Possibly from Shakespeare's *Romeo and Juliet*.

[24] Remonstrance or earnest and kindly protest.

[25] From *An Essay on Man* (1734) by Alexander Pope (1688–1744).

[26] *Mencius*, 6A:17.

[27] Excessive or ostentatious pride, especially in one's achievements.

bonum[28] of earthly existence. Fame, and not wealth or knowledge, was the goal toward which youths had to strive. Many a lad swore within himself as he crossed the threshold of his paternal home, that he would not recross it until he had made a name in the world; and many an ambitious mother refused to see her sons again unless they could "return home," as the expression is, "caparisoned in brocade."[29] To shun shame or win a name, samurai boys would submit to any privations and undergo severest ordeals of bodily or mental suffering. They knew that honor won in youth grows with age. In the memorable siege of Osaka,[30] a young son of Iyéyasu, in spite of his earnest entreaties to be put in the vanguard, was placed at the rear of the army. When the castle fell, he was so chagrined and wept so bitterly that an old councilor[31] tried to console him with all the resources at his command; "Take comfort, Sire," said he, "at the thought of the long future before you. In the many years that you may live, there will come divers[32] occasions to distinguish yourself." The boy fixed his indignant gaze upon the man and said—"How foolishly you talk! Can ever my fourteenth year come round again?" Life itself was thought cheap if honor and fame could be attained therewith: hence, whenever a cause presented itself which was considered dearer than life, with utmost serenity and celerity was life laid down.

Of the causes in comparison with which no life was too dear to sacrifice, was the duty of loyalty, which was the keystone making feudal virtues a symmetrical arch.

---

[28] "The highest good."

[29] Dressed in elaborate clothing indicating wealth and success.

[30] Tokugawa Ieyasu attacked Osaka Castle in the winter of 1614 and the summer of 1615 to destroy the Toyotomi legacy once and for all. This story concerns Ieyasu's tenth son, Tokugawa Yorinobu (1602–71).

[31] Matsudaira Masatsuna (1576–1648), a leading official who served the first two Tokugawa shoguns.

[32] Several or many.

CHAPTER IX

The Duty of Loyalty

Feudal morality shares other virtues in common with other systems of ethics, with other classes of people, but this virtue—homage and fealty to a superior—is its distinctive feature. I am aware that personal fidelity is a moral adhesion existing among all sorts and conditions of men—a gang of pickpockets owe allegiance to a Fagin;[1] but it is only in the code of chivalrous honor that loyalty assumes paramount importance.

In spite of Hegel's criticism[2] that the fidelity of feudal vassals, being an obligation to an individual and not to a commonwealth, is a bond established on totally unjust principles, a great compatriot of his made it his boast that personal loyalty was a German virtue. Bismarck had good reasons to do so, not because the *Treue*[3] he boasts of was the monopoly of his Fatherland or of any single nation or race, but because this favored fruit of chivalry lingers latest among the people where feudalism has lasted longest. In America, where "everybody is as good as anybody else," and, as the Irishman added,[4] "better too," such exalted ideas of loyalty as we feel for our sovereign may be deemed "excellent within certain bounds,"[5] but

---

[1] A character in Charles Dickens's novel *Oliver Twist* (1838) who controlled a group of child pickpockets.

[2] [*Philosophy of History* (Eng. trans. by Sibree), pt. IV, sec. ii, ch. i.] *Georg Wilhelm Friedrich Hegel (1770–1831)* was a German philosopher.

[3] Faithfulness or loyalty.

[4] Meant as an amusing reference to a stereotypical Irish habit of tongue.

[5] From Sir Walter Scott's novel *Woodstock or the Cavalier. A Tale of the Year Sixteen Hundred and Fifty-one* (1826).

preposterous as encouraged among us. Montesquieu[6] complained long ago that right on one side of the Pyrenees[7] was wrong on the other, and the recent Dreyfus trial proved the truth of his remark, save that the Pyrenees were not the sole boundary beyond which French justice finds no accord.[8] Similarly, loyalty as we conceive it may find few admirers elsewhere, not because our conception is wrong, but because it is, I am afraid, forgotten, and also because we carry it to a degree not reached in any other country. Griffis[9] was quite right in stating that whereas in China Confucian ethics made obedience to parents the primary human duty, in Japan precedence was given to loyalty. At the risk of shocking some of my good readers, I will relate of one "who could endure to follow a fall'n lord" and who thus, as Shakespeare assures, "earned a place i' the story."[10]

The story is of one of the greatest characters of our history, Michizané,[11] who, falling a victim to jealousy and calumny,[12] is exiled from the capital. Not content with this, his unrelenting enemies are now bent upon the extinction of his family. Strict search for his son—not yet grown—reveals the fact of his being secreted in a village school kept by one Genzo, a former vassal of Michizané. When orders are dispatched to the schoolmaster to deliver the head of the

---

[6] Nitobe mistakenly ascribes this "complaint" to Montesquieu. The correct source is Blaise Pascal (1623–62), a French mathematician and philosopher, in *Thoughts* (*Pensées*, 1670, "Krailsheimer" No. 294).

[7] A range of mountains in southwest Europe.

[8] Alfred Dreyfus (1859–1935), a French military officer who was falsely accused of treason in 1894. Although wrongly convicted for passing information to Germany, he was eventually cleared of all culpability in 1906.

[9] [*Religions of Japan.*] William Elliot Griffis (1843–1928). See footnote 15 in my introduction to this edition of Nitobe's *Bushido*. Griffis authored *The Religions of Japan from the Dawn of History to the Era of Meiji* (1895).

[10] Words by Domitius Enobarus in Shakespeare's *Antony and Cleopatra*.

[11] Sugawara-no-Michizane (845–903). Nitobe is referring to a famous 1746 puppet and Kabuki play, "*Sugawara Denjū Tenarai-kagami*" (Sugawara and the Secrets of Calligraphy).

[12] Slander.

juvenile offender on a certain day, his first idea is to find a suitable substitute for it. He ponders over his school-list, scrutinizes with careful eyes all the boys, as they stroll into the classroom, but none among the children born of the soil bears the least resemblance to his protégé. His despair, however, is but for a moment; for, behold, a new scholar is announced—a comely boy of the same age as his master's son, escorted by a mother of noble mien.[13]

No less conscious of the resemblance between infant lord and infant retainer, were the mother and the boy himself. In the privacy of home both had laid themselves upon the altar; the one his life— the other her heart, yet without sign to the outer world. Unwitting of what had passed between them, it is the teacher from whom comes the suggestion.

Here, then, is the scapegoat!—The rest of the narrative may be briefly told.—On the day appointed, arrives the officer commissioned to identify and receive the head of the youth. Will he be deceived by the false head? The poor Genzo's hand is on the hilt of the sword, ready to strike a blow either at the man or at himself, should the examination defeat his scheme. The officer takes up the gruesome object before him, goes calmly over each feature, and in a deliberate, businesslike tone, pronounces it genuine.—That evening in a lonely home awaits the mother we saw in the school. Does she know the fate of her child? It is not for his return that she watches with eagerness for the opening of the wicket.[14] Her father-in-law has been for a long time a recipient of Michizané's bounties, but since his banishment, circumstances have forced her husband to follow the service of the enemy of his family's benefactor. He himself could not be untrue to his own cruel master; but his son could serve the cause of the grandsire's lord. As one acquainted with the exile's family, it was he who had been entrusted with the

---

[13] Demeanor or character.

[14] A small door or gate.

task of identifying the boy's head. Now the day's—yea, the life's—
hard work is done, he returns home and as he crosses its threshold,
he accosts his wife, saying: "Rejoice, my wife, our darling son has
proved of service to his lord!"

"What an atrocious story!" I hear my readers exclaim. "Parents
deliberately sacrificing their own innocent child to save the life of
another man's!" But this child was a conscious and willing victim:
it is a story of vicarious[15] death—as significant as, and not more
revolting than, the story of Abraham's intended sacrifice of Isaac.[16]
In both cases was obedience to the call of duty, utter submission
to the command of a higher voice, whether given by a visible or
an invisible angel, or heard by an outward or an inward ear—but I
abstain from preaching.

The individualism of the West, which recognizes separate interests for father and son, husband and wife, necessarily brings
into strong relief the duties owed by one to the other; but Bushido
held that the interest of the family and of the members thereof is
intact—one and inseparable. This interest it bound up with affection—natural, instinctive, irresistible; hence, if we die for one we
love with natural love (which animals themselves possess), what is
that? "For if ye love them that love you, what reward have ye? Do
not even the publicans[17] the same?"[18]

In his great history, Sanyo[19] relates in touching language the

---

[15] Acting or serving as a substitute.

[16] As told in Genesis 22.

[17] Tax collector.

[18] Matthew 5:46.

[19] Rai San'yō (1780–1832), a Confucian scholar who wrote the influential 22-vol-
ume *Nihon Gaishi* (Unofficial History of Japan, 1826). Taira-no-Shigemori
(1138–79) was the eldest son of Taira-no-Kiyomori (1118–81). When Kiyo-
mori, who wielded considerable influence in court, heard rumor that the emperor was plotting against him, he pronounced his intention to attack
preemptively. Shigemori then informed his father that he would side with the
emperor come what may. As such, Shigemori became a celebrated figure in the

heart struggle of Shigemori concerning his father's rebellious conduct. "If I be loyal, my father must be undone; if I obey my father,
my duty to my sovereign must go amiss." Poor Shigemori! We see
him afterward praying with all his soul that kind Heaven may visit
him with death, that he may be released from this world where it
is hard for purity and righteousness to dwell.

Many a Shigemori has his heart torn by the conflict between
duty and affection. Indeed, neither Shakespeare nor the Old Testament itself contains an adequate rendering of *ko*, our conception of
filial piety, and yet in such conflicts Bushido never wavered in its
choice of loyalty. Women, too, encouraged their offspring to sacrifice all for the king. Even as resolute as Widow Windham and her
illustrious consort, the samurai matron stood ready to give up her
boys for the cause of loyalty.[20]

Since Bushido, like Aristotle[21] and some modern sociologists,
conceived the state as antedating[22] the individual—the latter being
born into the former as part and parcel thereof—he must live and
die for it or for the incumbent of its legitimate authority. Readers
of Crito[23] will remember the argument with which Socrates represents the laws of the city as pleading with him on the subject of his
escape. Among others he makes them (the laws or the state) say:
"Since you were begotten and nurtured and educated under us,
dare you once to say you are not our offspring and servant, you and

---

Meiji period because of his righteous loyalty to the emperor that exceeded filial piety.

[20] Anne Gerard, the wife of Sir Francis Windham (1612–76), the royalist who
gave sanctuary to Charles II of England before the monarch fled to France in
1651 while being pursued by Oliver Cromwell.

[21] Aristotle (c. 384–322 BC), a Greek philosopher acclaimed for being the founder of "logic."

[22] Preceding in time.

[23] *Crito* (360 BC) is a dialogue of the philosopher Plato (c. 429–c. 347 BC). Socrates
(c. 469–399 BC) is being held captive and rationalizes to his friend Crito why he
must obey Athenian law and take his own life instead of escaping.

your fathers before you?" These are words which do not impress us as anything extraordinary; for the same thing has long been on the lips of Bushido, with this modification, that the laws and the state were represented with us by a personal being. Loyalty is an ethical outcome of this political theory.

I am not entirely ignorant of Mr. Spencer's view according to which political obedience—loyalty—is accredited with only a transitional function.[24] It may be so. Sufficient unto the day is the virtue thereof. We may complacently repeat it, especially as we believe that day to be a long space of time, during which, so our national anthem says, "tiny pebbles grow into mighty rocks draped with moss."[25]

We may remember at this juncture that even among so democratic a people as the English, "the sentiment of personal fidelity to a man and his posterity which their Germanic ancestors felt for their chiefs, has," as Monsieur Boutmy recently said, "only passed more or less into their profound loyalty to the race and blood of their princes, as evidenced in their extraordinary attachment to the dynasty."

Political subordination, Mr. Spencer predicts, will give place to loyalty, to the dictates of conscience. Suppose his induction is realized—will loyalty and its concomitant instinct of reverence disappear forever? We transfer our allegiance from one master to another, without being unfaithful to either: from being subjects of a ruler that wields the temporal scepter[26] we become servants of the monarch who sits enthroned in the penetralia of our hearts.[27] A few years ago a very stupid controversy, started by the misguided disciples of

---

[24] [*Principles of Ethics*, vol. I, pt. ii, ch. x.]

[25] *Kimigayo*. The national anthem is a 31-syllable *waka* of the Heian period. Basil Hall Chamberlain translated it as follows: "Thousands of years of happy reign be thine; Rule on, my lord, till what are pebbles now; By age united to mighty rocks shall grow; Whose venerable sides the moss doth line." Although adopted for ceremonial occasions by the government in 1893, it only became the official national anthem of Japan in 1999.

[26] Fleeting royal or imperial authority.

[27] Innermost recesses of the heart.

Spencer, made havoc among the reading class of Japan. In their zeal to uphold the claim of the throne to undivided loyalty, they charged Christians with treasonable propensity in that they avow fidelity to their Lord and Master.[28] They arrayed forth sophistical arguments without the wit of Sophists,[29] and scholastic tortuosities[30] minus the niceties of the Schoolmen. Little did they know that we can, in a sense, "serve two masters without holding to the one or despising the other,"[31] "rendering unto Caesar the things that are Caesar's and unto God the things that are God's."[32] Did not Socrates, all the while he unflinchingly refused to concede one iota of loyalty to his daemon,[33] obey with equal fidelity and equanimity the command of his earthly master, the State? His conscience he followed, alive; his country he served, dying. Alack[34] the day when a state grows so powerful as to demand of its citizens the dictates of their conscience!

Bushido did not require us to make our conscience the slave of any lord or king. Thomas Mowbray was a veritable spokesman for us when he said:

> Myself I throw, dread sovereign, at thy foot.
> My life thou shall command, but not my shame.
> The one my duty owes; but my fair name,

---

[28] Perhaps alluding to the controversy in which his close friend Uchimura Kanzō (1861–1930) became embroiled in 1891. When he was a teacher at the First National School in Tokyo, Uchimura refused to bow before the emperor's signature affixed to a copy of the new Imperial Rescript on Education. This stance, along with his general disapproval of Japanese imperial expansion, brought Christianity under suspicion in the 1890s.

[29] The Sophists were Greek philosophers active from around the fifth century BC who taught rhetoric and proper conduct for living. The Schoolmen or Scholastics were medieval academics or philosophers.

[30] Something that is crooked.

[31] Matthew 6:24 and Luke 16:13.

[32] Matthew 22:21.

[33] A god.

[34] Exclamation of sorrow or dismay.

Despite of death, that lives upon my grave,
To dark dishonor's use, thou shall not have.[35]

A man who sacrificed his own conscience to the capricious will
or freak or fancy of a sovereign was accorded a low place in the
estimate of the Precepts.[36] Such a one was despised as *nei-shin*, a
cringeling, who makes court by unscrupulous fawning, or as *chô-
shin*, a favorite who steals his master's affections by means of servile
compliance; these two species of subjects corresponding exactly to
those which Iago describes—the one, a duteous and knee-crooking
knave, doting on his own obsequious bondage,[37] wearing out his
time much like his master's ass; the other trimming in forms and
visages of duty, keeping yet his heart attending on himself.[38] When
a subject differed from his master, the loyal path for him to pursue
was to use every available means to persuade him of his error, as
Kent did to King Lear.[39] Failing in this, let the master deal with him
as he wills. In cases of this kind, it was quite a usual course for the
samurai to make the last appeal to the intelligence and conscience
of his lord by demonstrating the sincerity of his words with the
shedding of his own blood.[40]

Life being regarded as the means whereby to serve his master,
and its ideal being set upon honor, the whole education and training of a samurai were conducted accordingly.

---

[35] Thomas Mowbray (1366–99) had a tumultuous relationship with King Richard
II (1367–1400) and was eventually banished to Venice. Nitobe is quoting from
Shakespeare's *Richard II*.

[36] Teachings of the Bible.

[37] Characterized by or showing servile deference.

[38] Shakespeare's *Othello*. Nitobe is quoting the passage where Iago is explaining
why he serves Othello.

[39] In Shakespeare's play *King Lear*, Kent is banished for defending the king's
daughter Cordelia from her father's bullying. Kent then dons the clothes of a
peasant still resolved to dutifully serve his king incognito.

[40] In other words, a protest of one's sincerity demonstrated through committing
seppuku.

CHAPTER X

The Education and Training of a Samurai

The first point to observe in knightly pedagogies was to build up character, leaving in the shade the subtler faculties of prudence, intelligence, and dialectics.[1] We have seen the important part aesthetic accomplishments played in his education. Indispensable as they were to a man of culture, they were accessories rather than essentials of samurai training. Intellectual superiority was, of course, esteemed; but the word *Chi*, which was employed to denote intellectuality, meant wisdom in the first instance and gave knowledge only a very subordinate place. The tripod which supported the framework of Bushido was said to be *Chi*, *Jin*, *Yu*, respectively, Wisdom, Benevolence, and Courage. A samurai was essentially a man of action. Science was without the pale of his activity. He took advantage of it in so far as it concerned his profession of arms. Religion and theology were relegated to the priests; he concerned himself with them in so far as they helped to nourish courage. Like an English poet the samurai believed "'tis not the creed that saves the man; but it is the man that justifies the creed."[2] Philosophy and literature formed the chief part of his intellectual training; but even in the pursuit of these, it was not objective

---

[1] Discourse or the art of discussion.

[2] Robert Bulwer-Lytton (1831–91), an English diplomat who composed poetry under the pseudonym Owen Meredith. Nitobe is quoting from Meredith's poem "The Wanderer."

truth that he strove after—literature was pursued mainly as a pas-time, and philosophy as a practical aid in the formation of charac-ter, if not for the exposition of some military or political problem.

From what has been said, it will not be surprising to note that the curriculum of studies, according to the pedagogies of Bushi-do, consisted mainly of the following—fencing, archery, *jiujutsu*[3] or *yawara*, horsemanship, the use of the spear, tactics, calligraphy, ethics, literature, and history. Of these, *jiujutsu* and calligraphy may require a few words of explanation. Great stress was laid on good writing, probably because our logograms,[4] partaking as they do of the nature of pictures, possess artistic value, and also because chirography[5] was accepted as indicative of one's personal charac-ter. *Jiujutsu* may be briefly defined as an application of anatomi-cal knowledge to the purpose of offense or defense. It differs from wrestling in that it does not depend upon muscular strength. It dif-fers from other forms of attack in that it uses no weapons. Its feat consists in clutching or striking such part of the enemy's body as will make him numb and incapable of resistance. Its object is not to kill, but to incapacitate one for action for the time being.

A subject of study which one would expect to find in military education and which is rather conspicuous by its absence in the Bushido course of instruction, is mathematics. This, however, can be readily explained in part by the fact that feudal warfare was not carried on with scientific precision. Not only that, but the whole training of the samurai was unfavorable to fostering numerical notions.

Chivalry is uneconomical: it boasts of penury.[6] It says with Ventidius that "ambition, the soldier's virtue, rather makes choice

---

[3] [The same word as that misspelled jiu-jitsu in common English parlance. It is the gentle art. It "uses no weapon." (W. E. G.)]

[4] Ideograms. Kanji.

[5] Penmanship or calligraphy.

[6] Extreme poverty.

of loss, than gain which darkens him."[7] Don Quixote[8] takes more pride in his rusty spear and skin-and-bones horse than in gold and lands, and a samurai is in hearty sympathy with his exaggerated confrère of La Mancha.[9] He disdains money itself—the art of making or hoarding it. It was to him veritably filthy lucre.[10] The hackneyed expression to describe the decadence of an age was "that the civilians loved money and the soldiers feared death."[11] Niggardliness[12] of gold and of life excited as much disapprobation[13] as their lavish use was panegyrized.[14] "Less than all things," says a current precept, "men must grudge money: it is by riches that wisdom is hindered." Hence children were brought up with utter disregard of economy. It was considered bad taste to speak of it, and ignorance of the value of different coins was a token of good breeding. Knowledge of numbers was indispensable in the mustering of forces as well as in distribution of benefices and fiefs; but the counting of money was left to meaner hands. In many feudatories, public finance was administered by a lower kind of samurai or by priests. Every thinking bushi knew well enough that money formed the sinews of war;[15] but he did not think of raising the appreciation of money to a virtue. It is true that thrift was enjoined by Bushido, but not for economical reasons so much as for the exercise of abstinence. Luxury was thought the greatest menace to manhood, and severest simplicity of living was required of the warrior class,

---

7 In Shakespeare's *Antony and Cleopatra*, Publius Ventidius (91–31 BC) was the great general who defeated the formidable Parthians.

8 Miguel de Cervantes's (1547–1616) classic novel *Don Quixote* (1605 and 1615).

9 A samurai could surely identify with his peer, Don Quixote of Le Mancha.

10 Monetary reward or gain.

11 Cited from Southern Song general Yue Fei's (1103–42) biography.

12 Miserly or begrudging.

13 The act or state of disapproval.

14 To praise highly.

15 Nitobe is citing Roman orator Cicero's (106–43 BC) *Philippics*. "Endless money forms the sinews of war."

sumptuary laws[16] being enforced in many of the clans.

We read that in ancient Rome the farmers of revenue and other financial agents were gradually raised to the rank of knights, the State thereby showing its appreciation of their service and of the importance of money itself. How closely this is connected with the luxury and avarice of the Romans may be imagined. Not so with the Precepts of Knighthood. It persisted in systematically regarding finance as something low—low as compared with moral and intellectual vocations.

Money and the love of it being thus diligently ignored, Bushido itself could long remain free from a thousand and one evils of which money is the root.[17] This is sufficient reason for the fact that our public men have long been free from corruption; but alas! how fast plutocracy is making its way in our time and generation.

The mental discipline, which would nowadays be chiefly aided by the study of mathematics, was supplied by literary exegesis and deontological[18] discussions. Very few abstract subjects troubled the mind of the young, the chief aim of their education being, as I have said, decision of character. People whose minds were simply stored with information found no great admirers. Of the three services of studies that Bacon gives—for delight, ornament, and ability—Bushido had decided preference for the last, where their use was "in judgment and the disposition of business."[19] Whether it was for the disposition of public business or for the exercise of self-control, it was with a practical end in view that education was conducted. "Learning without thought," said Confucius, "is labor lost; thought without learning is perilous."[20]

---

[16] Rules to regulate expenditure.

[17] Timothy 6:10.

[18] Deontology is the theory or study of moral obligation.

[19] Francis Bacon (1561–1626). Nitobe cites Bacon's "On Studies" (1597).

[20] *Analects*, 2:15.

When character and not intelligence, when the soul and not the head, is chosen by a teacher for the material to work upon and to develop, his vocation partakes of a sacred character. "It is the parent who has borne me: it is the teacher who makes me man." With this idea, therefore, the esteem in which one's preceptor[21] was held was very high. A man to evoke such confidence and respect from the young, must necessarily be endowed with superior personality, without lacking erudition. He was a father to the fatherless, and an adviser to the erring. "Thy father and thy mother"—so runs our maxim—"are like heaven and earth; thy teacher and thy lord are like the sun and moon."[22]

The present system of paying for every sort of service was not in vogue among the adherents of Bushido. It believed in a service which can be rendered only without money and without price. Spiritual service, be it of priest or teacher, was not to be repaid in gold or silver, not because it was valueless but because it was invaluable. Here the nonarithmetical honor instinct of Bushido taught a truer lesson than modern Political Economy; for wages and salaries can be paid only for services whose results are definite, tangible, and measurable, whereas the best service done in education— namely, in soul development (and this includes the services of a pastor), is not definite, tangible, or measurable. Being immeasurable, money, the ostensible measure of value, is of inadequate use. Usage sanctioned that pupils brought to their teachers money or goods at different seasons of the year; but these were not payments but offerings, which indeed were welcome to the recipients as they were usually men of stern caliber, boasting of honorable penury, too dignified to work with their hands and too proud to beg. They

---

[21] Teacher, tutor or headmaster of a school.

[22] A precept quoted from Jitsugokyō, an important textbook studied by Japanese children from medieval through to modern times. It was learned in tandem with Dōjikyō, which contained moral teachings.

were grave personifications of high spirits undaunted by adversity. They were an embodiment of what was considered as an end of all learning, and were thus a living example of that discipline of disciplines, self-control, which was universally required of samurai.

CHAPTER XI

Self-Control

The discipline of fortitude on the one hand, inculcating endurance without a groan, and the teaching of politeness on the other, requiring us not to mar the pleasure or serenity of another by expressions of our own sorrow or pain, combined to engender a stoical turn of mind and eventually to confirm it into a national trait of apparent stoicism. I say apparent stoicism, because I do not believe that true stoicism can ever become the characteristic of a whole nation, and also because some of our national manners and customs may seem to a foreign observer hard-hearted. Yet we are really as susceptible to tender emotion as any race under the sky.

I am inclined to think that in one sense we have to feel more than others—yes, doubly more—since the very attempt to restrain natural promptings entails suffering. Imagine boys—and girls, too—brought up not to resort to the shedding of a tear or the uttering of a groan for the relief of their feelings—and there is a physiological problem whether such effort steels their nerves or makes them more sensitive.

It was considered unmanly for a samurai to betray his emotions on his face. "He shows no sign of joy or anger,"[1] was a phrase used, in describing a great character. The most natural affections were kept under control. A father could embrace his son only at the expense of his dignity; a husband would not kiss his wife—no, not in the presence of other people, whatever he might do in private! There may

---

[1] This expression is found in the first chapter of prominent Meiji educator Fukuzawa Yukichi's autobiographical work, *Fuku-ō Jiden* (1899).

be some truth in the remark of a witty youth when he said, "American husbands kiss their wives in public and beat them in private;
Japanese husbands beat theirs in public and kiss them in private."

Calmness of behavior, composure of mind, should not be disturbed by passion of any kind. I remember when, during the late
war with China, a regiment left a certain town, a large concourse of
people flocked to the station to bid farewell to the general and his
army.[2] On this occasion an American resident resorted to the place,
expecting to witness loud demonstrations, as the nation itself was
highly excited and there were fathers, mothers, wives, and sweet-
hearts of the soldiers in the crowd. The American was strangely
disappointed;[3] for as the whistle blew and the train began to move,
the hats of thousands of people were silently taken off and their
heads bowed in reverential farewell; no waving of handkerchiefs, no
word uttered, but deep silence in which only an attentive ear could
catch a few broken sobs. In domestic life, too, I know of a father who
spent whole nights listening to the breathing of a sick child, standing behind the door that he might not be caught in such an act of
parental weakness![4] I know of a mother who, in her last moments,
refrained from sending for her son, that he might not be disturbed
in his studies.[5] Our history and everyday life are replete with examples of heroic matrons who can well bear comparison with some
of the most touching pages of Plutarch.[6] Among our peasantry an
Ian Maclaren would be sure to find many a Marget Howe.[7]

---

[2] The First Sino-Japanese War of 1894–95. It has been suggested that Nitobe is
referring to his own family in the following account.

[3] Perhaps Mary.

[4] Perhaps Nitobe himself.

[5] Nitobe's mother Seki.

[6] Plutarch (c. AD 45–c. 120), a Greek philosopher who authored *Parallel Lives*
and *Moralia* among others.

[7] Ian Maclaren was the pseudonym for Scottish minister John Watson (1850–
1907). In his novel *Beside the Bonnie Briar Bush* (1894), Marget Howe is depicted as an exemplary mother to her son.

It is the same discipline of self-restraint which is accountable for the absence of more frequent revivals in the Christian churches of Japan. When a man or woman feels his or her soul stirred, the first instinct is quietly to suppress the manifestation of it. In rare instances is the tongue set free by an irresistible spirit, when we have eloquence of sincerity and fervor. It is putting a premium upon a breach of the third commandment to encourage speaking lightly of spiritual experience.[8] It is truly jarring to Japanese ears to hear the most sacred words, the most secret heart experiences, thrown out in promiscuous audiences. "Dost thou feel the soil of thy soul stirred with tender thoughts? It is time for seeds to sprout. Disturb it not with speech; but let it work alone in quietness and secrecy"—writes a young samurai in his diary.[9]

To give in so many articulate words one's inmost thoughts and feelings—notably the religious—is taken among us as an unmistakable sign that they are neither very profound nor very sincere. "Only a pomegranate is he"—so runs a popular saying "who, when he gapes his mouth, displays the contents of his heart."[10]

It is not altogether perverseness of oriental minds that the instant our emotions are moved, we try to guard our lips in order to hide them. Speech is very often with us, as the Frenchman defines it, "the art of concealing thought."[11]

Call upon a Japanese friend in time of deepest affliction and he will invariably receive you laughing, with red eyes or moist cheeks. At first you may think him hysterical. Press him for explanation and you will get a few broken commonplaces—"Human life has sorrow"; "They who meet must part"; "He that is born must die";

---

[8] Exodus 20:7. Third Commandment: "Thou shalt not take the name of the Lord in vain."

[9] Perhaps from Nitobe's own diary.

[10] When ripe, the outer skin of a pomegranate ruptures revealing its bright red innards.

[11] Charles Maurice de Talleyrand-Périgord (1754–1838), a French diplomat.

"It is foolish to count the years of a child that is gone, but a woman's heart will indulge in follies"; and the like. So the noble words of a noble Hohenzollern[12]—"Lerne zu leiden ohne klagen"—had found many responsive minds among us long before they were uttered.[13]

Indeed, the Japanese have recourse to risibility whenever the frailties of human nature are put to severest test. I think we possess a better reason than Democritus[14] himself for our Abderian[15] tendency, for laughter with us most often veils an effort to regain balance of temper when disturbed by any untoward circumstance. It is a counterpoise of sorrow or rage.

The suppression of feelings being thus steadily insisted upon, they find their safety-valve in poetical aphorisms. A poet of the tenth century[16] writes "In Japan and China as well, humanity, when moved by sorrow, tells its bitter grief in verse." A mother who tries to console her broken heart by fancying her departed child absent on his wonted chase after the dragonfly hums,

How far today in chase, I wonder,
Has gone my hunter of the dragonfly![17]

I refrain from quoting other examples, for I know I could do only scant justice to the pearly gems of our literature, were I to ren-

---

[12] The ruling house of Brandenburg-Prussia (1415–1918) and imperial Germany (1871–1918).

[13] Frederick III (1831–88), son of Emperor William I of Germany. Frederick replaced his father, as emperor in 1888 but died shortly after. Nitobe misquotes the German phrase (*Lerne leiden, ohne zu klagen*), which means "Learn to suffer without complaint."

[14] Democritus (c. 460–c. 370 BC), a Greek philosopher who was referred to as the "laughing philosopher."

[15] Abden was Democritus's place of birth.

[16] Ki-no-Tsurayuki (c. 868–c. 945), a poet and compiler of the *Kokinshū* (Collection of Ancient and Modern Poetry, 905). Nitobe is quoting a section from *Tosa Nikki* (Tosa Diary, 935).

[17] Supposedly a verse composed by the woman poet Kaga-no-Chiyojo (1703–75).

der into a foreign tongue the thoughts which were wrung drop by drop from bleeding hearts and threaded into beads of rarest value. I hope I have in a measure shown that inner working of our minds which often presents an appearance of callousness or of a hysterical mixture of laughter and dejection, and whose sanity is sometimes called in question.

It has also been suggested that our endurance of pain and indifference to death are due to less sensitive nerves. This is plausible as far as it goes. The next question is—why are our nerves less tightly strung? It may be our climate is not so stimulating as the American. It may be our monarchical form of government does not excite us so much as the Republic does the Frenchman. It may be that we do not read *Sartor Resartus* so zealously as the Englishman. Personally, I believe it was our very excitability and sensitiveness which made it a necessity to recognize and enforce constant self-repression; but whatever may be the explanation, without taking into account long years of discipline in self-control, none can be correct.

Discipline in self-control can easily go too far. It can well repress the genial current of the soul. It can force pliant natures into distortions and monstrosities. It can beget bigotry, breed hypocrisy, or hebetate affections.[18] Be a virtue never so noble, it has its counterpart and counterfeit. We must recognize in each virtue its own positive excellence and follow its positive ideal, and the ideal of self-restraint is to keep the mind level—as our expression is—or, to borrow a Greek term, attain the state of *euthymia*,[19] which Democritus called the highest good.

The acme[20] and pitch of self-control is reached and best illustrated in the first of the two institutions which we shall now bring to view, namely, the institutions of suicide and redress.

---

[18] To make dull or blunt.

[19] Cheerfulness or tranquility.

[20] The highest point.

CHAPTER XII

The Institutions of Suicide and Redress[1]

O
f these two institutions (the former known as *hara-kiri* and the latter as *kataki-uchi*), many foreign writers have treated more or less fully.

To begin with suicide, let me state that I confine my observations only to *seppuku* or *kappuku*, popularly known as *hara-kiri*—which means self-immolation by disembowelment. "Ripping the abdomen? How absurd!"—so cry those to whom the name is new. Absurdly odd as it may sound at first to foreign ears, it cannot be so very foreign to students of Shakespeare, who puts these words in Brutus's mouth—"Thy [Caesar's] spirit walks abroad and turns our swords into our proper entrails."[2] Listen to a modern English poet who, in his *Light of Asia*, speaks of a sword piercing the bowels of a queen—none blames him for bad English or breach of modesty.[3] Or, to take still another example, look at Guercino's painting of Cato's death[4] in the Palazzo Rossa[5] in Genoa. Whoever has

---

[1] Vendetta or act of revenge.

[2] Shakespeare's *Julius Caesar*. Marcus Junius Brutus (85–42 BC) was one of the Roman senators who murdered Julius Caesar. Brutus was to later commit suicide when defeated by Octavian and Marcus Antonius at the Battle of Philippi.

[3] Edwin Arnold (1832–1904), a British journalist and poet whose book, *The Light of Asia* (1879), was about the life of Buddha.

[4] Giovanni Francesco Barbieri (1591–1666), an Italian painter. Cato the Younger (Marcus Porcius Cato Uticensis, 95–46 BC) was a Roman statesman who opposed Julius Caesar and eventually took his own life after fleeing to Utica.

[5] Palazzo Rosso, an historical palace in Genoa built in 1677.

read the swan-song which Addison[6] makes Cato sing will not jeer at the sword half-buried in his abdomen. In our minds this mode of death is associated with instances of noblest deeds and of most touching pathos, so that nothing repugnant, much less ludicrous, mars our conception of it. So wonderful is the transforming power of virtue, of greatness, of tenderness, that the vilest form of death assumes a sublimity and becomes a symbol of new life, or else— the sign which Constantine beheld would not conquer the world![7]

Not for extraneous associations only does *seppuku* lose in our mind any taint of absurdity; for the choice of this particular part of the body to operate upon was based on an old anatomical belief as to the seat of the soul and of the affections. When Moses wrote of Joseph's "bowels yearning upon his brother,"[8] or David prayed the Lord not to forget his bowels,[9] or when Isaiah,[10] Jeremiah,[11] and other inspired men of old spoke of the "sounding" or the "troubling" of bowels, they all and each endorsed the belief prevalent among the Japanese that in the abdomen was enshrined the soul. The Semites habitually spoke of the liver and kidneys and surrounding fat as the seat of emotion and of life. The term "*hara*"[12] was more comprehensive than the Greek *phren* or *thumos*, and the Japanese and Hellenese alike thought the spirit of man to dwell somewhere in that region. Such a notion is by no means confined to the peoples of antiquity. The French, in spite of the theory propounded by one

---

[6] Joseph Addison (1672–1719), an English playwright and politician. He wrote the play *Cato: A Tragedy* in 1712, depicting the hero Cato as a paragon of virtue. "Swan-song" is the final act.

[7] The sign being the cross of Christ used in his crucifixion. Constantine (c. 274–337) became the Roman empire's first Christian emperor, making Christianity the state religion in 324.

[8] Genesis 23:30.

[9] Psalms 26:6.

[10] Isaiah 63:15.

[11] Jeremiah 31–20.

[12] Japanese word for belly.

of their most distinguished philosophers, Descartes,[13] that the soul
is located in the pineal gland,[14] still insist in using the term *ventre*
in a sense which, if anatomically too vague, is nevertheless physi-
ologically significant. Similarly, *entrailles* stands in their language
for affection and compassion. Nor is such a belief mere superstition,
being more scientific than the general idea of making the heart the
center of the feelings. Without asking a friar, the Japanese knew better than Romeo "in what vile part of this anatomy one's name did
lodge."[15] Modern neurologists speak of the abdominal and pelvic
brains, denoting thereby sympathetic nerve centers in those parts
which are strongly affected by any psychical action. This view of
mental physiology once admitted, the syllogism[16] of *seppuku* is easy
to construct. "I will open the seat of my soul and show you how it
fares with it. See for yourself whether it is polluted or clean."

I do not wish to be understood as asserting religious or even
moral justification of suicide, but the high estimate placed upon
honor was ample excuse with many for taking one's own life. How
many acquiesced in the sentiment expressed by Garth,[17]

> When honor's lost, 'tis a relief to die;
> Death's but a sure retreat from infamy,

and have smilingly surrendered their souls to oblivion! Death in-
volving a question of honor was accepted in Bushido as a key to the
solution of many complex problems, so that to an ambitious samurai

---

[13] René Descartes (1596–1650), French philosopher and scientist who is credited
with coining the phrase "I think, therefore I am."

[14] Source of melatonin.

[15] Shakespeare's *Romeo and Juliet*. The forlorn Romeo threatens to kill himself
with his dagger in Friar Laurence's cell.

[16] Logical argument.

[17] Samuel Garth (1661–1719), an English physician and poet. Nitobe is citing his
poem "*The Dispensary*" (1699).

a natural departure from life seemed a rather tame affair and a con-
summation not devoutly to be wished for. I dare say that many good
Christians, if only they are honest enough, will confess the fascina-
tion of, if not positive admiration for, the sublime composure with
which Cato, Brutus, Petronius,[18] and a host of other ancient worthies
terminated their own earthly existence. Is it too bold to hint that the
death of the first of the philosophers was partly suicidal?[19] When we
are told so minutely by his pupils how their master willingly sub-
mitted to the mandate of the state—which he knew was morally
mistaken—in spite of the possibilities of escape, and how he took
the cup of hemlock in his own hand, even offering libation from
its deadly contents, do we not discern, in his whole proceeding and
demeanor, an act of self-immolation? No physical compulsion here,
as in ordinary cases of execution. True, the verdict of the judges was
compulsory: it said, "Thou shalt die—and that by thine own hand."
If suicide meant no more than dying by one's own hand, Socrates
was a clear case of suicide. But nobody would charge him with the
crime; Plato, who was averse to it, would not call his master a suicide.

Now my readers will understand that *seppuku* was not a mere
suicidal process. It was an institution, legal and ceremonial. An
invention of the middle ages, it was a process by which warriors
could expiate their crimes, apologize for errors, escape from disgrace, redeem their friends, or prove their sincerity. When enforced
as a legal punishment, it was practiced with due ceremony. It was a
refinement of self-destruction, and none could perform it without
the utmost coolness of temper and composure of demeanor, and for
these reasons it was particularly befitting the profession of bushi.

Antiquarian curiosity, if nothing else, would tempt me to give

---

[18] Gaius Petronius Arbiter (c. 27–66), a Roman writer who was assigned by Nero
(37–68) to be his "arbiter of taste." He took his own life when he was errone-
ously charged with planning to kill the emperor.

[19] The Greek philosopher Socrates (469–399 BC) killed himself when accused of
heresy and adversely influencing the minds of Athenian youth.

here a description of this obsolete ceremony; but seeing that such
a description was made by a far abler writer, whose book is not
much read nowadays, I am tempted to make a somewhat lengthy
quotation. Mitford,[20] in his *Tales of Old Japan*, after giving a translation of a treatise on *seppuku* from a rare Japanese manuscript,
goes on to describe an instance of such an execution of which he
was an eyewitness:

> We (seven foreign representatives) were invited to fol-
> low the Japanese witnesses into the *hondo* or main hall
> of the temple, where the ceremony was to be performed.
> It was an imposing scene. A large hall with a high roof
> supported by dark pillars of wood. From the ceiling
> hung a profusion of those huge gilt lamps and orna-
> ments peculiar to Buddhist temples. In front of the high
> altar, where the floor, covered with beautiful white mats,
> is raised some three or four inches from the ground, was
> laid a rug of scarlet felt. Tall candles placed at regular
> intervals gave out a dim mysterious light, just sufficient
> to let all the proceedings be seen. The seven Japanese
> took their places on the left of the raised floor, the seven
> foreigners on the right. No other person was present.
>
> After the interval of a few minutes of anxious sus-
> pense, Taki Zenzaburo,[21] a stalwart man thirty-two years
> of age, with a noble air, walked into the hall attired in his

---

[20] Algernon Bertram Freeman-Mitford (1837–1916), a British diplomat who came
to Japan after a posting in China in 1866. He wrote *Tales of Old Japan* (1871).

[21] The Kobe Incident of February 4, 1868, was the first international diplomatic
incident faced by the new Meiji government after the Restoration. Taki Zenzaburo was in charge of the third cannon group of Bizen troops who came across
two French sailors in Sannomiya. Zenzaburo tried to stop them going further,
but neither side could communicate effectively so a skirmish broke out. Nobody was killed, but incensed foreign powers forced the execution of Taki Zenzaburo to send a message. Zenzaburo was simply following orders.

dress of ceremony, with the peculiar hempen-cloth wings which are worn on great occasions. He was accompanied by a *kaishaku* and three officers, who wore the *jimbaori* or war surcoat with gold tissue facings. The word *kaishaku*, it should be observed, is one to which our word executioner is no equivalent term. The office is that of a gentleman; in many cases it is performed by a kinsman or friend of the condemned, and the relation between them is rather that of principal and second than that of victim and executioner. In this instance, the *kaishaku* was a pupil of Taki Zenzaburo, and was selected by friends of the latter from among their own number for his skill in swordsmanship.

With the *kaishaku* on his left hand, Taki Zenzaburo advanced slowly toward the Japanese witnesses, and the two bowed before them, then drawing near to the foreigners they saluted us in the same way, perhaps even with more deference; in each case the salutation was ceremoniously returned. Slowly and with great dignity the condemned man mounted on to the raised floor, prostrated himself before the high altar twice, and seated[22] himself on the felt carpet with his back to the high altar, the *kaishaku* crouching on his left-hand side. One of the three attendant officers then came forward, bearing a stand of the kind used in the temple for offerings, on which, wrapped in paper, lay the *wakizashi*, the short sword or dirk of the Japanese, nine inches and a half in length, with a point and an edge as sharp as a razor's. This he handed, prostrating himself, to the condemned man, who received it reverently raising it to his head

---

[22] [Seated himself—that is, in the Japanese fashion, his knees and toes touching the ground and his body resting on his heels. In this position, which is one of respect, he remained until his death.]

with both hands, and placed it in front of himself.

After another profound obeisance, Taki Zenzaburo, in a voice which betrayed just so much emotion and hesitation as might be expected from a man who is making a painful confession, but with no sign of either in his face or manner, spoke as follows:—

"I, and I alone, unwarrantably gave the order to fire on the foreigners at Kobe, and again as they tried to escape. For this crime I disembowel myself, and I beg you who are present to do me the honor of witnessing the act."

Bowing once more, the speaker allowed his upper garments to slip down to his girdle, and remained naked to the waist. Carefully, according to custom, he tucked his sleeves under his knees to prevent himself from falling backward; for a noble Japanese gentleman should die falling forwards. Deliberately, with a steady hand he took the dirk that lay before him; he looked at it wistfully, almost affectionately; for a moment he seemed to collect his thoughts for the last time, and then stabbing himself deeply below the waist in the left-hand side, he drew the dirk slowly across to his right side, and turning it in the wound, gave a slight cut upwards. During this sickeningly painful operation he never moved a muscle of his face. When he drew out the dirk, he leaned forward and stretched out his neck; an expression of pain for the first time crossed his face, but he uttered no sound. At that moment the *kaishaku*, who, still crouching by his side, had been keenly watching his every movement, sprang to his feet, poised his sword for a second in the air; there was a flash, a heavy, ugly thud, a crashing fall; with one blow the head had been severed from the body.

A dead silence followed, broken only by the hideous noise of the blood throbbing out of the inert heap before us, which but a moment before had been a brave and chivalrous man. It was horrible.

The *kaishaku* made a low bow, wiped his sword with a piece of paper which he had ready for the purpose, and retired from the raised floor; and the stained dirk was solemnly borne away, a bloody proof of the execution. The two representatives of the Mikado then left their places, and crossing over to where the foreign witness-es sat, called to us to witness that the sentence of death upon Taki Zenzaburo had been faithfully carried out. The ceremony being at an end, we left the temple.

I might multiply any number of descriptions of *seppuku* from literature or from the relations of eyewitnesses; but one more instance will suffice.

Two brothers, Sakon and Naiki, respectively twenty-four and seventeen years of age, made an effort to kill Iyéyasu in order to avenge their father's wrongs; but before they could enter the camp they were made prisoners. The old general admired the pluck of the youths who dared an attempt on his life and ordered that they should be allowed to die an honorable death. Their little brother Hachimaro, a mere infant of eight summers, was condemned to a similar fate, as the sentence was pronounced on all the male members of the family, and the three were taken to a monastery where it was to be executed. A physician who was present on the occasion has left us a diary, from which the following scene is translated:

When they were all seated in a row for final dispatch, Sakon turned to the youngest and said—"Go thou first, for I wish to be sure that thou doest it aright." Upon the little one's replying that, as he had never seen *seppuku* performed, he would like to see his brothers do it and then he could follow them, the older brothers smiled between their tears:—"Well said, little fellow! So canst thou well boast of being our father's child." When they had placed him between them, Sakon thrust the dagger into the left side of his abdomen and said—"Look brother! Dost understand now? Only, don't push the dagger too far, lest thou fall back. Lean forward, rather, and keep thy knees well composed." Naiki did likewise and said to the boy—"Keep thine eyes open or else thou mayst look like a dying woman. If thy dagger feels anything within and thy strength fails, take courage and double thy effort to cut across." The child looked from one to the other, and, when both had expired, he calmly half denuded himself and followed the example set him on either hand.

The glorification of *seppuku* offered, naturally enough, no small temptation to its unwarranted committal. For causes entirely incompatible with reason, or for reasons entirely undeserving of death, hot-headed youths rushed into it as insects fly into fire; mixed and dubious motives drove more samurai to this deed than nuns into convent gates. Life was cheap—cheap as reckoned by the popular standard of honor. The saddest feature was that honor, which was always in the *agio*,[23] so to speak, was not always solid gold, but alloyed with baser metals. No one circle in the Inferno will boast of greater density of Japanese population than the seventh, to which Dante consigns all victims of self-destruction![24]

And yet, for a true samurai to hasten death or to court it was alike cowardice. A typical fighter, when he lost battle after battle and was pursued from plain to hill and from bush to cavern, found himself hungry and alone in the dark hollow of a tree, his sword

---

[23] Currency exchange.

[24] The seventh circle of Dante's *Inferno* is that of Violence: Against Neighbors, Against Self (Wood of Suicides), Against God Art, and Nature. Fourteenth-century poem by Dante Alighieri describing Dante's journey through Hell.

blunt with use, his bow broken and arrows exhausted—did not the noblest of the Romans fall upon his own sword in Philippi under like circumstances?[25]—deemed it cowardly to die, but, with a fortitude approaching a Christian martyr's, cheered himself with an impromptu verse:

> Come! evermore come,
>> Ye dread sorrows and pains!
> And heap on my burden'd back;
> That I not one test may lack
>> Of what strength in me remains![26]

This, then, was the Bushido teaching—bear and face all calamities and adversities with patience and a pure conscience; for, as Mencius[27] taught, "When Heaven is about to confer a great office on anyone, it first exercises his mind with suffering and his sinews and bones with toil; it exposes his body to hunger and subjects him to extreme poverty: and it confounds his undertakings. In all these ways it stimulates his mind, hardens his nature, and supplies his incompetencies." True honor lies in fulfilling Heaven's decree, and no death incurred in so doing is ignominious, whereas, death to avoid what Heaven has in store is cowardly indeed! In that quaint book of Sir Thomas Browne's,[28] *Religio Medici*, there is an exact English equivalent for what is repeatedly taught in our Precepts. Let me quote it: "It is a brave act of valor to contemn death, but where life is more terrible than death, it is then the truest valor to

---

[25] Brutus.

[26] Yamanaka Yukimori (1540–78), a warrior who served the Izumo domain and then later Toyotomi Hideyoshi.

[27] [I use Dr. Legge's translation verbatim.] *Mencius*, 6B:15.

[28] Thomas Browne (1605–82), an English physician and writer whose autobiographical *Religio Medici* (The Religion of a Physician), written in 1643, was a popular read in its day.

dare to live." A renowned priest of the seventeenth century satiri-
cally observed—"Talk as he may, a samurai who ne'er has died is
apt in decisive moments to flee or hide."[29] Again—"Him who once
has died in the bottom of his breast, no spears of Sanada nor all
the arrows of Tametomo can pierce."[30] How near we come to the
portals of the temple whose Builder taught "He that loseth his life
for my sake shall find it"![31] These are but a few of the numerous
examples that tend to confirm the moral identity of the human
species, notwithstanding an attempt so assiduously made to render
the distinction between Christian and Pagan as great as possible.

We have thus seen that the Bushido institution of suicide was
neither so irrational nor barbarous as its abuse strikes us at first
sight. We will now see whether its sister institution of Redress—
or call it Revenge, if you will—has its mitigating features. I hope I
can dispose of this question in a few words, since a similar institution, or call it custom, if that suits you better, prevailed among all
peoples and has not yet become entirely obsolete, as attested by the
continuance of dueling and lynching. Why, has not an American
captain recently challenged Esterhazy, that the wrongs of Dreyfus
be avenged?[32] Among a savage tribe which has no marriage, adul-
tery is not a sin, and only the jealousy of a lover protects a woman
from abuse; so in a time which has no criminal court, murder is
not a crime, and only the vigilant vengeance of the victim's people preserves social order. "What is the most beautiful thing on
earth?" said Osiris to Horus.[33] The reply was, "To avenge a parent's

---

[29] Perhaps the Tendai Buddhist monk Tenkai (1536–1643).

[30] Sanada Yukimura (1567–1615) and Minamoto-no-Tametomo (1139–70) were
warriors famous for their fighting prowess using the spear and the bow.

[31] Matthew 10:39.

[32] Alfred Dreyfus. See Chapter IX, footnote 8. Marie Charles Ferdinand Walsin
Esterhazy (1847–1923) was the officer who confessed to carrying out the crime.

[33] An ancient Egyptian myth where Horus avenges his father Osirus's murder by his
uncle, Seth. Although dead, Osirus appears before Horus and asks this question.

wrongs"—to which a Japanese would have added "and a master's."

In revenge there is something which satisfies one's sense of justice. The avenger reasons—"My good father did not deserve death. He who killed him did great evil. My father, if he were alive, would not tolerate a deed like this: Heaven itself hates wrongdoing. It is the will of my father; it is the will of Heaven that the evil-doer ceases from his work. He must perish by my hand; because he shed my father's blood, I, who am his flesh and blood, must shed the murderer's. The same Heaven shall not shelter him and me." The ratiocination[34] is simple and childish (though we know Hamlet did not reason much more deeply); nevertheless it shows an innate sense of exact balance and equal justice. "An eye for an eye, a tooth for a tooth."[35] Our sense of revenge is as exact as our mathematical faculty, and until both terms of the equation are satisfied, we cannot get over the sense of something left undone.

In Judaism, which believed in a jealous God, or in Greek mythology, which provided a Nemesis, vengeance may be left to superhuman agencies; but common sense furnished Bushido with the institution of redress as a kind of ethical court of equity, where people could take cases not to be judged in accordance with ordinary law. The master of the forty-seven Ronins was condemned to death;[36] he had no court of higher instance to appeal to; his faithful retainers addressed themselves to vengeance, the only Supreme Court existing; they in their turn were condemned by common

---

[34] The process of exact thinking or reasoning.

[35] Exodus 21:24, Leviticus 24:20, Deuteronomy 19:21.

[36] Asano Naganori (1667–1701), a *daimyō* of the Akō domain who was ordered to commit suicide for drawing his sword against Kira Yoshinaka (1641–1702) inside the shogun's Edo Castle. Believing their lord was unfairly treated, Asano's 47 retainers avenged his death by attacking Kira's mansion and transporting his severed head to Asano's grave at Sengakuji Temple. Instead of being executed like common criminals for their unauthorized vendetta, 46 of the retainers were permitted to commit *seppuku*, an honorable death, and were enshrined next to their lord. The lone survivor was sent back to Akō to inform the people of the domain.

law—but the popular instinct passed a different judgment, and hence their memory is still kept as green and fragrant as are their graves at Sengakuji to this day.

Though Lâo-tse[37] taught to recompense injury with kindness, the voice of Confucius was very much louder, which taught that injury must be recompensed with justice[38]—and yet revenge was justified only when it was undertaken on behalf of our superiors and benefactors. One's own wrongs, including injuries done to wife and children, were to be borne and forgiven. A samurai could therefore fully sympathize with Hannibal's oath to avenge his country's wrongs,[39] but he scorns James Hamilton for wearing in his girdle a handful of earth from his wife's grave, as an eternal incentive to avenge her wrongs on the Regent Murray.[40]

Both of these institutions of suicide and redress lost their *raison d'être* at the promulgation of the Criminal Code.[41] No more do we hear of romantic adventures of a fair maiden as she tracks in disguise the murderer of her parent. No more can we witness tragedies of family vendetta enacted. The knight errantry of Miyamoto Musashi is now a tale of the past.[42] The well-ordered police spies out the criminal for the injured party and the law metes out

---

[37] Laozi (Lao Tse, J: Rōshi, 6th century BC), an ancient Chinese philosopher considered to be the founder of Taoism. Nitobe may be citing from Section 63 of the text *Laozi*.

[38] *Analects*, 14:36.

[39] Hannibal (247–182 BC), a Carthaginian general who attacked Italy by traversing the alps in the Second Punic War (218–201 BC). Hannibal apparently swore an oath to his father before departing from Sicily for Iberia in 237 BC.

[40] James Hamilton (c. 1531–1581), a Scottish supporter of Mary, Queen of Scots (1542–87). He assassinated James Stewart, 1st Earl of Moray in 1570. According to a possibly fictionalized account by Sir Walter Scott, Hamilton killed Stewart and his party because James Bellenden evicted Hamilton's wife and child in the middle of the night and they froze to death.

[41] The Code of Criminal Instruction and the Penal Code were issued in 1880.

[42] Miyamoto Musashi (1582–1645), one of the greatest Japanese swordsmen of all time. Known for fighting with two swords simultaneously, his book *Gorin-no-sho* (Book of Five Rings) is still influential in modern Japanese martial arts.

justice. The whole state and society will see that wrong is righted. The sense of justice satisfied; there is no need of *kataki-uchi*. If this had meant that "hunger of the heart which feeds upon the hope of glutting that hunger with the life blood of the victim," as a New England divine has described it, a few paragraphs in the Criminal Code would not so entirely have made an end of it.

As to *seppuku*, though it too has no *existence de jure*,[43] we still hear of it from time to time, and shall continue to hear, I am afraid, as long as the past is remembered. Many painless and time-saving methods of self-immolation will come in vogue, as its votaries are increasing with fearful rapidity throughout the world; but Professor Morselli will have to concede to *seppuku* an aristocratic position among them. He maintains that "when suicide is accomplished by very painful means or at the cost of prolonged agony, in ninety-nine cases out of a hundred, it may be assigned as the act of a mind disordered by fanaticism, by madness, or by morbid excitement."[44] But a normal *seppuku* does not savor of fanaticism, or madness or excitement, utmost *sang froid*[45] being necessary to its successful accomplishment. Of the two kinds into which Dr. Strahan[46] divides suicide, the Rational or Quasi, and the Irrational or True, *seppuku* is the best example of the former type.

From these bloody institutions, as well as from the general tenor of Bushido, it is easy to infer that the sword played an important part in social discipline and life. The saying passed as an axiom which called the sword the soul of the samurai.

---

[43] Not recognized as a legal institution.

[44] [Morselli, *Suicide*, p. 314.] Augostino Morselli (1852–1929) was an Italian medical professor at the University of Turin and the author of *Suicide: An Essay on Comparative Moral Statistics* (1882).

[45] Coolness of mind or calmness under pressure.

[46] [*Suicide and Insanity*.] Samuel Alexander Kenny Strahan (?–1902) was a British barrister and the author of *Suicide and Insanity: A Physiological and Sociological Study* (1893).

CHAPTER XIII

The Sword, the Soul
of the Samurai

B ushido made the sword its emblem of power and prowess. When Mahomet proclaimed that "the sword is the key of Heaven and of Hell,"[1] he only echoed a Japanese sentiment. Very early the samurai boy learned to wield it. It was a momentous occasion for him when at the age of five he was appareled in the paraphernalia of samurai costume, placed upon a *go*-board[2] and initiated into the rights of the military profession, by having thrust into his girdle a real sword instead of the toy dirk with which he had been playing. After this first ceremony of *adoptio per arma*,[3] he was no more to be seen outside his father's gates without this badge of his status, even though it was usually substituted for everyday wear by a gilded wooden dirk. Not many years pass before he wears constantly the genuine steel, though blunt, and then the sham arms are thrown aside and with enjoyment keener than his

---

[1] Muhammad (c. 570–632), prophet and founder of Islam. Nitobe's citation may have been retrieved from Edward Gibbon's *The History of the Decline and Fall of the Roman Empire* (1776–88).

[2] [The game of *go* is sometimes called Japanese checkers, but is much more intricate than the English game. The *go*-board contains 361 squares and is supposed to represent a battlefield—the object of the game being to occupy as much space as possible.]

[3] "Adoption by arms." A ceremony of induction for men-of-arms. Nitobe is alluding to his own childhood right of passage here.

newly acquired blades, he marches out to try their edge on wood and stone. When he reaches man's estate, at the age of fifteen, being given independence of action, he can now pride himself upon the possession of arms sharp enough for any work. The very possession of the dangerous instrument imparts to him a feeling and an air of self-respect and responsibility. "He beareth not the sword in vain."[4] What he carries in his belt is a symbol of what he carries in his mind and heart—loyalty and honor. The two swords, the longer and the shorter—called respectively *daito* and *shoto* or *katana* and *wakizashi*—never leave his side. When at home, they grace the most conspicuous place in the study or parlor; by night they guard his pillow within easy reach of his hand. Constant companions, they are beloved, and proper names of endearment given them. Being venerated, they are well-nigh worshipped. The Father of History has recorded as a curious piece of information that the Scythians[5] sacrificed to an iron scimitar.[6] Many a temple and many a family in Japan hoard a sword as an object of adoration. Even the commonest dirk has due respect paid to it. Any insult to it is tantamount to personal affront. Woe to him who carelessly steps over a weapon lying on the floor!

So precious an object cannot long escape the notice and the skill of artists nor the vanity of its owner, especially in times of peace, when it is worn with no more use than a crosier[7] by a bishop or a

---

[4] Romans 13:4.

[5] A group of ancient Indo-Persian people who excelled in mounted warfare and metallurgy.

[6] "The Father of History" is a reference to the Greek historian Herodotus (5th century BC). This observation by Nitobe is alluding to his seminal work, *Histories* Book IV, where the dagger's sacrificial role is described. "An antique iron sword is planted on the top of every such mound, and serves as the image of Mars: yearly sacrifices of cattle and of horses are made to it, and more victims are offered thus than to all the rest of their gods."

[7] A staff carried by a high-ranking priest.

scepter by a king. Sharkskin and finest silk for hilt, silver and gold for guard, lacquer of varied hues for scabbard, robbed the deadliest weapon of half its terror; but these appurtenances[8] are playthings compared with the blade itself.

The swordsmith was not a mere artisan but an inspired artist and his workshop a sanctuary. Daily he commenced his craft with prayer and purification, or, as the phrase was, "he committed his soul and spirit into the forging and tempering of the steel." Every swing of the sledge, every plunge into water, every friction on the grindstone was a religious act of no slight import. Was it the spirit of the master or of his tutelary god that cast a formidable spell over our sword? Perfect as a work of art, setting at defiance it's Toledo and Damascus rivals,[9] there was more than art could impart. Its cold blade, collecting on its surface the moment it is drawn the vapor of the atmosphere; its immaculate texture, flashing light of bluish hue; its matchless edge, upon which histories and possibilities hang; the curve of its back, uniting exquisite grace with utmost strength—all these thrill us with mixed feelings of power and beauty, of awe and terror. Harmless were its mission, if it only remained a thing of beauty and joy! But, ever within reach of the hand, it presented no small temptation for abuse. Too often did the blade flash forth from its peaceful sheath. The abuse sometimes went so far as to try the acquired steel on some harmless creature's neck.

The question that concerns us most is, however—Did Bushido justify the promiscuous use of the weapon? The answer is unequivocally, no! As it laid great stress on its proper use, so did it denounce and abhor its misuse. A dastard or a braggart was he who brandished his weapon on undeserved occasions. A self-possessed man knows the right time to use it, and such times come but rarely. Let

---

[8] Accessories.

[9] Toledo and Damascus were famous for their steel and swords.

us listen to the late Count Katsu,[10] who passed through one of the most turbulent times of our history, when assassinations, suicides, and other sanguinary practices were the order of the day. Endowed as he once was with almost dictatorial powers, chosen repeatedly as an object of assassination, he never tarnished his sword with blood. In relating some of his reminiscences to a friend he says, in a quaint, plebeian way peculiar to him: "I have a great dislike for killing people and so I haven't killed one single man. I have released those whose heads should have been chopped off. A friend said to me one day, 'You don't kill enough. Don't you eat pepper and egg-plants?' Well, some people are no better! But you see that fellow was slain himself. My escape may be due to my dislike of killing. I had the hilt of my sword so tightly fastened to the scabbard that it was hard to draw the blade. I made up my mind that though they cut me, I would not cut. Yes, yes! Some people are truly like fleas and mosquitoes and they bite—but what does their biting amount to? It itches a little, that's all; it won't endanger life."[11] These are the words of one whose Bushido training was tried in the fiery furnace of adversity and triumph. The popular apothegm[12]—"To be beaten is to conquer," meaning true conquest consists in not opposing a riotous foe; and "The best won victory is that obtained without shedding of blood," and others of similar import—will show that after all the ultimate ideal of knighthood was peace.

---

[10] Katsu Kaishū (1823–99), a high-ranking shogunate official who sailed the *Kanrin Maru* to the United States in 1860. Following the important role he played in negotiating the surrender of Edo Castle to the imperial loyalists during the 1868 Meiji Restoration, Kaishū became an influential statesman in the new Meiji government.

[11] Citation from *Kaishū Yoha* (1899), a book written by educator Iwamoto Yoshi-haru (1863–1942). The friend mentioned by Kaishū is Kawakami Kensai (1834–72). A fervent xenophobe staunchly opposed to opening Japan to the West, he was executed after murdering two government officials. Nitobe inexplicably replaces pumpkin (kabocha) in the original Japanese as pepper.

[12] A short instructive saying.

It was a great pity that this high ideal was left exclusively to priests and moralists to preach, while the samurai went on practicing and extolling martial traits. In this they went so far as to tinge the ideals of womanhood with Amazonian character. Here we may profitably devote a few paragraphs to the subject of the training and position of woman.

CHAPTER XIV

The Training and Position of Woman

The female half of our species has sometimes been called
the paragon of paradoxes, because the intuitive working
of its mind is beyond the comprehension of men's "ar-
ithmetical understanding." The Chinese ideogram denoting "the
mysterious,"[1] "the unknowable," consists of two parts, one meaning "young" and the other "woman," because the physical charms
and delicate thoughts of the fair sex are above the coarse mental
caliber of our sex to explain.

In the Bushido ideal of woman, however, there is little mystery
and only a seeming paradox. I have said that it was Amazonian,
but that is only half the truth. Ideographically the Chinese represent wife by a woman holding a broom[2]—certainly not to brandish
it offensively or defensively against her conjugal ally, neither for
witchcraft, but for the more harmless uses for which the besom
was first invented—the idea involved being thus not less homely
than the etymological derivation of the English wife (weaver) and
daughter (*duhitar*, milkmaid). Without confining the sphere of
woman's activity to *Küche, Kirche, Kinder*, as the present German
Kaiser is said to do,[3] the Bushido ideal of womanhood was pre-

[1] 女+少＝妙
[2] 女+帚＝婦
[3] "Kitchen, Church and Children." Referred to as the "Three Ks," this slogan was
gaining popularity in Germany when Nitobe was studying there.

eminently domestic. These seeming contradictions—domesticity
and Amazonian traits—are not inconsistent with the Precepts of
Knighthood, as we shall see.

Bushido being a teaching primarily intended for the masculine
sex, the virtues it prized in woman were naturally far from being
distinctly feminine. Winckelmann[4] remarks that "the supreme
beauty of Greek art is rather male than female," and Lecky adds
that it was true in the moral conception of the Greeks as in their
art. Bushido similarly praised those women most "who emanci-
pated themselves from the frailty of their sex and displayed a heroic
fortitude worthy of the strongest and the bravest of men."[5] Young
girls, therefore, were trained to repress their feelings, to indurate
their nerves, to manipulate weapons—especially the long-handled
sword called *nagi-nata*[6]—so as to be able to hold their own against
unexpected odds. Yet the primary motive for exercise of this martial character was not for use in the field; it was twofold—personal
and domestic. Woman owning no suzerain of her own, formed
her own bodyguard. With her weapon she guarded her personal
sanctity with as much zeal as her husband did his master's. The
domestic utility of her warlike training was in the education of her
sons, as we shall see later.

Fencing and similar exercises, if rarely of practical use, were a
wholesome counterbalance to the otherwise sedentary habits of
women. But these exercises were not followed only for hygienic
purposes. They could be turned into use in times of need. Girls,
when they reached womanhood, were presented with dirks (*kai-
ken*, pocket poniards)[7], which might be directed to the bosom of
their assailants, or, if advisable, to their own. The latter was very

---

[4] Johann Joachim Winckelmann (1717–68), a German historian who published
The History of Ancient Art in 1763.

[5] [Lecky, *History of European Morals*, ii, p. 383.]

[6] A glaive.

[7] A small dagger.

often the case; and yet I will not judge them severely. Even the
Christian conscience, with its horror of self-immolation, will not
be harsh with them, seeing Pelagia[8] and Dominina,[9] two suicides,
were canonized for their purity and piety. When a Japanese Virginia[10] saw her chastity menaced, she did not wait for her father's
dagger. Her own weapon lay always in her bosom. It was a disgrace
to her not to know the proper way in which she had to perpetrate
self-destruction. For example, little as she was taught in anatomy,
she must know the exact spot to cut in her throat; she must know
how to tie her lower limbs together with a belt so that, whatever the
agonies of death might be, her corpse be found in utmost modesty
with the limbs properly composed. Is not a caution like this worthy
of the Christian Perpetua or the Vestal Cornelia?[11] I would not put
such an abrupt interrogation were it not for a misconception, based
on our bathing customs and other trifles, that chastity is unknown
among us.[12] On the contrary, chastity was a preeminent virtue of
the samurai woman, held above life itself. A young woman, taken
prisoner, seeing herself in danger of violence at the hands of the
rough soldiery, says she will obey their pleasure, provided she is
first allowed to write a line to her sisters, whom war has dispersed
in every direction. When the epistle is finished, off she runs to the
nearest well and saves her honor by drowning. The letter she leaves

---

[8] Pelagia was a 15-year-old Christian girl who jumped from her rooftop to avoid
being raped during the Syrian Diocletianic Persecution of AD 303.

[9] Perhaps the Christian martyr Saint Domnina from Antioch who was arrested
by soldiers for her faith. Afraid that she and her two daughters would be raped,
they threw themselves into a river and drowned in AD 310.

[10] Virginia was killed by her father to prevent her suffering the humiliation of
being seduced by Crassinus, a corrupt Roman official.

[11] Perpetua was a young Christian woman martyred for her beliefs in Rome. Cornelia was a "Vestal Virgin," a maiden who attended the Roman goddess Vesta.
She was buried alive at the order of the notorious tyrant Domitian in AD 90
after being wrongly indicted for losing her chastity.

[12] [For a very sensible explanation of nudity and bathing, see Finck's *Lotos Time
in Japan*, pp. 286–97.]

behind ends with these verses:

> For fear lest clouds may dim her light,
> Should she but graze this nether sphere,
> The young moon poised above the height
> Doth hastily betake to flight.[13]

It would be unfair to give my readers an idea that masculinity alone was our highest ideal for woman. Far from it! Accomplishments and the gentler graces of life were required of them. Music, dancing, and literature were not neglected. Some of the finest verses in our literature were expressions of feminine sentiments; in fact, woman played an important role in the history of Japanese *belles-lettres*.[14] Dancing was taught (I am speaking of samurai girls and not of geisha) only to smooth the angularity of their movements. Music was to regale the weary hours of their fathers and husbands; hence it was not for the technique, the art as such, that music was learned; for the ultimate object was purification of heart, since it was said that no harmony of sound is attainable without the player's heart being in harmony with itself. Here again we see the same idea prevailing which we notice in the training of youths—that accomplishments were ever kept subservient to moral worth. Just enough of music and dancing to add grace and brightness to life, but never to foster vanity and extravagance. I sympathize with the Persian Prince, who, when taken into a ballroom in London and asked to take part in the merriment, bluntly remarked that in his country they provided a particular set of girls to do that kind of business for them.

The accomplishments of our women were not acquired for

---

[13] A parting poem by the wife of Torii Yoshichirō. Her father and husband were slain in battle against Oda Nobunaga in 1573.

[14] Literature regarded as fine art, especially that with a purely aesthetic function.

show or social ascendancy. They were a home diversion; and if they shone in social parties, it was as the attributes of a hostess—in other words, as a part of the household contrivance for hospitality. Domesticity guided their education. It may be said that the accomplishments of the women of Old Japan, be they martial or pacific in character, were mainly intended for the home; and, however far they might roam, they never lost sight of the hearth as the center. It was to maintain its honor and integrity that they slaved, drudged, and gave up their lives. Night and day, in tones at once firm and tender, brave and plaintive, they sang to their little nests. As daughter, woman sacrificed herself for her father, as wife for her husband, and as mother for her son. Thus from earliest youth she was taught to deny herself. Her life was not one of independence, but of dependent service. Man's helpmeet,[15] if her presence is helpful she stays on the stage with him: if it hinders his work, she retires behind the curtain. Not infrequently does it happen that a youth becomes enamored of a maiden who returns his love with equal ardor, but, when she realizes his interest in her makes him forgetful of his duties, disfigures her person that her attractions may cease. Adzuma,[16] the ideal wife in the minds of samurai girls, finds herself loved by a man who is conspiring against her husband. Upon pretence of joining in the guilty plot, she manages in the dark to take her husband's place, and the sword of the lover-assassin descends upon her own devoted head. The following epistle written by the wife of a young *daimio*,[17] before taking her own life, needs no comment:

---

[15] Genesis 2:18. "And the Lord God said, It is not good that the man should be alone; I will make him an help [helper] for him."

[16] Adzuma may be alluding to Atoma from the chronicle *Genpei Jōsuiki* about war between the Minamoto and the Taira (1180–85).

[17] Kimura Shigenari (1592?–1615), a *daimyō* of the Nagato domain who served under Toyotomi Hideyori (Hideyoshi's son). He was killed in the Summer Siege of Osaka Castle defending it against the forces of Tokugawa Ieyasu. His wife apparently committed suicide beforehand so that Shigenari would not have any regrets about dying.

I have heard that no accident or chance ever mars the march of events here below, and that all is in accordance with a plan. To take shelter under a common bough or a drink of the same river, is alike ordained from ages prior to our birth. Since we were joined in ties of eternal wedlock, now two short years ago, my heart hath followed thee, even as its shadow followeth an object, inseparably bound heart to heart, loving and being loved. Learning but recently, however, that the coming battle is to be the last of thy labor and life, take the farewell greeting of thy loving partner. I have heard that Kowu,[18] the mighty warrior of ancient China, lost a battle, loth to part with his favorite Gu. Yoshinaka,[19] too, brave as he was, brought disaster to his cause, too weak to bid prompt farewell to his wife. Why should I, to whom earth no longer offers hope or joy—Why should I detain thee or thy thoughts by living? Why should I not, rather, await thee on the road which all mortal kind must sometime tread? Never, prithee,[20] never, forget that many benefits which our good master Hidéyori hath heaped upon thee. The gratitude we owe him is as deep as the sea and as high as the hills.

---

[18] Xiang Yu (232–202 BC), a military leader of Chu who helped topple the Qin Dynasty (221–206 BC). He was later beaten by the Han dynasty founder, Emperor Gaozu (256 or 247–195 BC). Xiang Yu's concubine took her own life much like Shigenari's wife so that Xiang Yu would not be sidetracked in his war against Gaozu (aka Liu Bang).

[19] Minamoto-no-Yoshinaka (1154–84), Minamoto-no-Yoritomo's cousin who seized the capital in 1183 forcing the Taira out. He essentially turned the Taira-Minamoto conflict into a triangular affair and fought against his own kin as well, but was eventually taken down by Minamoto-no-Yoshitsune and Minamoto-no-Yorinori (1156–1193).

[20] Pray thee.

Woman's surrender of herself to the good of her husband, home, and family was as willing and honorable as the man's self-surrender to the good of his lord and country. Self-renunciation, without which no life-enigma can be solved, was the keynote of the loyalty of man as well as of the domesticity of woman. She was no more the slave of man than was her husband of his liege-lord, and the part she played was recognized as *naijo*, "the inner help." In the ascending scale of service stood woman, who annihilated herself for man, that he might annihilate himself for the master, that he in turn might obey Heaven. I know the weakness of this teaching and that the superiority of Christianity is nowhere more manifested than here, in that it requires of each and every living soul direct responsibility to its Creator. Nevertheless, as far as the doctrine of service—the serving of a cause higher than one's own self, even at the sacrifice of one's individuality; I say the doctrine of service, which is the greatest that Christ preached and was the sacred keynote of His mission—so far as that is concerned, Bushido was based on eternal truth.

My readers will not accuse me of undue prejudice in favor of slavish surrender of volition. I accept in a large measure the view advanced and defended with breadth of learning and profundity of thought by Hegel, that history is the unfolding and realization of freedom. The point I wish to make is that the whole teaching of Bushido was so thoroughly imbued with the spirit of self-sacrifice, that it was required not only of woman but of man. Hence, until the influence of its precepts is entirely done away with, our society will not realize the view rashly expressed by an American exponent of woman's rights, who exclaimed, "May all the daughters of Japan rise in revolt against ancient customs!" Can such a revolt succeed? Will it improve the female status? Will the rights they gain by such a summary process repay the loss of that sweetness of disposition, that gentleness of manner, which are their present heritage? Was not the loss of domesticity on the part of Roman matrons followed

by moral corruption too gross to mention? Can the American re-
former assure us that a revolt of our daughters is the true course
for their historical development to take? These are grave questions.
Changes must and will come without revolts! In the meantime let
us see whether the status of the fair sex under the Bushido regimen
was really so bad as to justify a revolt.

We hear much of the outward respect European knights paid
to "God and the ladies"[21]—the incongruity of the two terms making Gibbon blush; we are also told by Hallam[22] that the morality of
chivalry was coarse, that gallantry implied illicit love. The effect of
chivalry on the weaker vessel was food for reflection on the part of
philosophers, M. Guizot[23] contending that feudalism and chivalry
wrought wholesome influences, while Mr. Spencer tells us that in
a militant society (and what is feudal society if not militant?) the
position of woman is necessarily low, improving only as society
becomes more industrial. Now is M. Guizot's theory true of Japan,
or is Mr. Spencer's? In reply I might aver that both are right. The
military class in Japan was restricted to the samurai, comprising
nearly two million souls. Above them were the military nobles, the
daimio, and the court nobles, the *kugé*—these higher, sybaritic[24]
nobles being fighters only in name. Below them were masses of the
common people—mechanics, tradesmen, and peasants—whose
life was devoted to arts of peace. Thus what Herbert Spencer gives
as the characteristics of a militant type of society may be said to
have been exclusively confined to the samurai class, while those of
the industrial type were applicable to the classes above and below

---

[21] Edward Gibbon (1737–94), an English historian who wrote *Decline and Fall of
the Roman Empire* (1776–88). He grudgingly makes reference to the knight as
"Champion of God and the ladies."

[22] Henry Hallam (1777–1859), an English historian and the author of *The View
of the State of Europe during the Middle Ages* (1880).

[23] François Guizot (1787–1874), a French historian and royalist.

[24] Partial to luxury or sensuous pleasure.

it. This is well illustrated by the position of woman; for in no class did she experience less freedom than among the samurai. Strange to say, the lower the social class—as, for instance, among small artisans—the more equal was the position of husband and wife. Among the higher nobility, too, the difference in the relations of the sexes was less marked, chiefly because there were few occasions to bring the differences of sex into prominence, the leisurely nobleman having become literally effeminate. Thus Spencer's dictum was fully exemplified in Old Japan. As to Guizot's, those who read his presentation of a feudal community will remember that he had the higher nobility especially under consideration, so that his generalization applies to the *daimio* and the *kugé*.

I shall be guilty of gross injustice to historical truth if my words give one a very low opinion of the status of woman under Bushido. I do not hesitate to state that she was not treated as man's equal; but, until we learn to discriminate between differences and inequalities, there will always be misunderstandings upon this subject.

When we think in how few respects men are equal among themselves, e.g., before law courts or voting polls, it seems idle to trouble ourselves with a discussion on the equality of sexes. When the American Declaration of Independence[25] said that all men were created equal, it had no reference to their mental or physical gifts; it simply repeated what Ulpian[26] long ago announced, that before the law all men are equal. Legal rights were in this case the measure of their equality. Were the law the only scale by which to measure the position of woman in a community, it would be as easy to tell where she stands as to give her avoirdupois in pounds and ounc-

---

[25] Paragraph 2 in the American Declaration of Independence (1776) states: "We hold these truths to be self-evident, that all men are created equal, that they are endowed by their Creator with certain unalienable Rights, that among these are Life, Liberty and the pursuit of Happiness."

[26] Ulpian (c. AD 170–223), a Roman jurist whose works influenced the promulgation of the *Corpus Juris Civilis* (Body of Civil Law, AD 529–34).

es. But the question is: Is there a correct standard in comparing the relative social position of the sexes? Is it right, is it enough, to compare woman's status to man's, as the value of silver is compared with that of gold, and give the ratio numerically? Such a method of calculation excludes from consideration the most important kind of value which a human being possesses, namely, the intrinsic. In view of the manifold variety of requisites for making each sex fulfill its earthly mission, the standard to be adopted in measuring its relative position must be of a composite character; or to borrow from economic language, it must be a multiple standard. Bushido had a standard of its own and it was binomial. It tried to gauge the value of woman on the battlefield and by the hearth. There she counted for very little; here for all. The treatment accorded her corresponded to this double measurement—as a social-political unit not much, while as wife and mother she received highest respect and deepest affection. Why, among so military a nation as the Romans, were their matrons so highly venerated? Was it not because they were *matrona*, mothers? Not as fighters or lawgivers, but as their mothers did men bow before them. So with us. While fathers and husbands were absent in field or camp, the government of the household was left entirely in the hands of mothers and wives. The education of the young, even their defense, was entrusted to them. The warlike exercises of women, of which I have spoken, were primarily to enable them intelligently to direct and follow the education of their children.

I have noticed a rather superficial notion prevailing among half-informed foreigners, that because the common Japanese expression for one's wife is "my rustic wife" and the like, she is despised and held in little esteem. When it is told that such phrases as "my foolish father," "my swinish son," "my awkward self," etc., are in current use, is not the answer clear enough?[27]

---

[27] Once common disparaging terms in Japan to express humility to outsiders.

To me it seems that our idea of marital union goes in some ways farther than the so-called Christian. "Man and woman shall be one flesh."[28] The individualism of the Anglo-Saxon cannot let go of the idea that husband and wife are two persons—hence when they disagree, their separate rights are recognized, and when they agree, they exhaust their vocabulary in all sorts of silly pet names and nonsensical blandishments. It sounds highly irrational to our ears, when a husband or wife speaks to a third party of his or her other half—better or worse—as being lovely, bright, kind, and what not. Is it good taste to speak of one's self as "my bright self," "my lovely disposition," and so forth? We think praising one's own wife is praising a part of one's own self, and self-praise is regarded, to say the least, as bad taste among us—and I hope, among Christian nations too! I have diverged at some length because the polite debasement of one's consort was a usage most in vogue among the samurai.

The Teutonic races beginning their tribal life with a superstitious awe of the fair sex (though this is really wearing off in Germany!), and the Americans beginning their social life under the painful consciousness of the numerical insufficiency of women[29] (who, now increasing, are, I am afraid, fast losing the prestige their colonial mothers enjoyed), the respect man pays to woman has in Western civilization become the chief standard of morality. But in the martial ethics of Bushido, the main watershed dividing the good and the bad was sought elsewhere. It was located along the line of duty which bound man to his own divine soul and then to other souls in the five relations[30] I have mentioned in the early part of this paper. Of these, we have brought to our reader's notice loy-

---

[28] Matthew 19:3-6.

[29] [I refer to those days when girls were imported from England and given in marriage for so many pounds of tobacco, etc.]

[30] Five relations of Confucianism: parent and child (affection), ruler and follower (righteousness), husband and wife (differentiation), elder and younger siblings (precedence), friend and friend (trust).

alty, the relation between one man as vassal and another as lord. Upon the rest, I have only dwelt incidentally as occasion presented itself; because they were not peculiar to Bushido. Being founded on natural affections, they could but be common to all mankind, though in some particulars they may have been accentuated by conditions which its teachings induced. In this connection there comes before me the peculiar strength and tenderness of friendship between man and man, which often added to the bond of brother-hood a romantic attachment doubtless intensified by the separation of the sexes in youth—a separation which denied to affection the natural channel open to it in Western chivalry or in the free inter-course of Anglo-Saxon lands. I might fill pages with Japanese ver-sions of the story of Damon and Pythias or Achilles and Patroclos, or tell in Bushido parlance of ties as sympathetic as those which bound David and Jonathan.[31]

It is not surprising, however, that the virtues and teachings unique in the Precepts of Knighthood did not remain circum-scribed to the military class. This makes us hasten to the consider-ation of the influence of Bushido on the nation at large.

---

[31] According to Greek mythology, Dionisius sentenced Pythias to be executed because of sedition. His friend Damon volunteered to be incarcerated in his place as a guarantee while Pythias took care of his affairs before death. In the *Illiad*, Achilles returns to fight in the Trojan war upon hearing of the death of his friend Patroclos, who disguised himself as the almighty Achilles to rouse the troops. In Samuel 17–20 of the Bible. Even though he was his rival to the throne, King Saul's oldest son Jonathan enters a covenant with David after he slayed the giant Goliath. "Jonathan became one in spirit with David, and he loved him as himself." Saul sees David as a threat to the crown and seeks to kill him, but Jonathan helps David escape.

CHAPTER XV

The Influence
of Bushido

T hus far we have brought into view only a few of the more prominent peaks which rise above the range of knightly virtues, in themselves so much more elevated then the general level of our national life. As the sun in its rising first tips the highest peaks with russet hue, and then gradually casts its rays on the valley below, so the ethical system which first enlightened the military order drew in course of time followers from amongst the masses. Democracy raises up a natural prince for its leader, and aristocracy infuses a princely spirit among the people. Virtues are no less contagious than vices. "There needs but one wise man in a company, and all are wise, so rapid is the contagion," says Emerson.[1] No social class or caste can resist the diffusive power of moral influence.

Prate[2] as we may of the triumphant march of Anglo-Saxon liberty, rarely has it received impetus from the masses. Was it not rather the work of the squires and gentlemen? Very truly does M. Taine[3] say, "These three syllables, as used across the channel, summarize the history of English society." Democracy may make

---

[1] Ralph Waldo Emerson (1803–82), an American philosopher and poet. Nitobe cites *Representative Men* (1850).

[2] To utter in empty or foolish talk.

[3] Hippolyte Adolphe Taine (1828–93), a French historian. Nitobe's quotation is from *Notes on England* (1872).

self-confident retorts to such a statement and fling back the question—[4] "When Adam delved and Eve span, where then was the
gentleman?" All the more pity that a gentleman was not present
in Eden! The first parents missed him sorely and paid a high price
for his absence. Had he been there, not only would the garden have
been more tastefully dressed, but they would have learned without
painful experience that disobedience to Jehovah was disloyalty and
dishonor, treason, and rebellion.

What Japan was she owed to the samurai. They were not only
the flower of the nation, but its root as well. All the gracious gifts
of Heaven flowed through them. Though they kept themselves so-
cially aloof from the populace, they set a moral standard for them
and guided them by their example. I admit Bushido had its esoteric
and exoteric teachings;[5] these were eudemonic,[6] looking after the
welfare and happiness of the commonalty; those were aretaic,[7] em-
phasizing the practice of virtues for their own sake.

In the most chivalrous days of Europe, knights formed numeri-
cally but a small fraction of the population, but, as Emerson says—
"In English literature half the drama and all the novels, from Sir
Philip Sidney[8] to Sir Walter Scott,[9] paint this figure (gentleman)."
Write in place of Sidney and Scott, Chikamatsu[10] and Bakin, and you
have in a nutshell the main features of the literary history of Japan.

The innumerable avenues of popular amusement and instruction—the theaters, the storytellers' booths, the preacher's dais, the
musical recitations, the novels—have taken for their chief theme

---

[4] An old nursery rhyme attributed to the priest John Ball (c. 1338–81) about the
     1381 Peasants' Revolt.
[5] Secret and open teachings.
[6] Conducive to happiness.
[7] Of or pertaining to virtue or excellence.
[8] Sir Philip Sidney (1554–16), an Elizabethan poet and soldier.
[9] Sir Walter Scott (1771–1832), a Scottish writer.
[10] Chikamatsu Monzaemon (1653–1725), a famous Japanese playwright espe-
     cially prominent in the world of *bunraku* puppet theater.

the stories of the samurai. The peasants around the open fire in their huts never tire of repeating the achievements of Yoshitsuné and his faithful retainer Benkéi,[11] or of the two brave Soga brothers;[12] the dusky urchins listen with gaping mouths until the last stick burns out and the fire dies in its embers, still leaving their hearts aglow with the tale that is told. The clerks and the shopboys, after their day's work is over and the *amado*[13] of the store are closed, gather together to relate the story of Nobunaga and Hidéyoshi far into the night, until slumber overtakes their weary eyes and transports them from the drudgery of the counter to the exploits of the field. The very babe just beginning to toddle is taught to lisp the adventures of Momotaro,[14] the daring conqueror of ogreland. Even girls are so imbued with the love of knightly deeds and virtues that, like Desdemona,[15] they would seriously incline to devour with greedy ear the romance of the samurai.

The samurai grew to be the *beau ideal*[16] of the whole race. "As among flowers the cherry is queen, so among men the samurai is lord," so sang the populace.[17] Debarred from commercial pursuits,

---

[11] Minamoto-no-Yoshitsune (1159–89), half-brother of the founder of the first warrior government, Minamoto-no-Yoritomo. Turned upon by Yoritomo who was suspicious of his brother's popularity and intentions, Yoshitsune was assailed and ended up committing suicide. His demise, together with that of his loyal follower, the *naginata*-wielding warrior monk Benkei (1155?– 89), made Yoshitsune one of Japan's most celebrated tragic heroes.

[12] The Soga brothers, Sukenari (1172–93) and Tokimune (1174–93), avenged their father's murderer, Kudō Suketsune, an act of filial piety that was made popular in the medieval chronicle *Soga Monogatari* (The Tale of the Soga Brothers).

[13] [Outside shutters.]

[14] Momotarō (Peach Boy) is the protagonist from a popular medieval Japanese folktale in which he leads a dog, a monkey and a pheasant into battle against ogres.

[15] Desdemona is the wife of Othello in Shakespeare's play, who is unfairly suspected of infidelity.

[16] The perfect type or model.

[17] The iconoclastic Zen priest Ikkyū (1394–1481) wrote the poem "Among men

the military class itself did not aid commerce, but there was no channel of human activity, no avenue of thought, which did not receive in some measure an impetus from Bushido. Intellectual and moral Japan was directly or indirectly the work of Knighthood.

Mr. Mallock,[18] in his exceedingly suggestive book, *Aristocracy and Evolution*, has eloquently told us that "social evolution, in so far as it is other than biological, may be defined as the unintended result of the intentions of great men"; further, that historical progress is produced by a struggle "not among the community generally, to live, but a struggle amongst a small section of the community to lead, to direct, to employ, the majority in the best way." Whatever may be said about the soundness of his argument, these statements are amply verified in the part played by bushi in the social progress, so far as it went, of our Empire.

How the spirit of Bushido permeated all social classes is also shown in the development of a certain order of men, known as *oto-ko-daté*,[19] the natural leaders of democracy. Staunch fellows were they, every inch of them strong with the strength of massive manhood. At once the spokesmen and the guardians of popular rights, they had each a following of hundreds and thousands of souls who proffered, in the same fashion that samurai did to *daimio*, the willing service of "limb and life, of body, chattels, and earthly honor."[20] Backed by a vast multitude of rash and impetuous working men, these born "bosses" formed a formidable check to the rampancy of

---

the samurai [is best]; among pillars, cypress wood; among fish, the sea bream; among robes, magenta; and among cherry blossoms, those of Yoshino."

[18] William Hurelle Mallock (1849–1913), an English writer. Nitobe's quote is from Aristocracy *and Evolution: A Study of the Rights, the Origin, and the Social Function of the Wealthier Classes* (1898).

[19] "Manly fellows," or "street heroes." Often masterless samurai who stood up for the underdog.

[20] From an oath of fealty to the King of England recorded in English clergyman William Stubbs's (1825–1901) *The Constitutional History of England, in Its Origin and Development* (1874–78).

the two-sworded order.

In manifold ways has Bushido filtered down from the social class where it originated, and acted as leaven among the masses, furnishing a moral standard for the whole people. The Precepts of Knighthood, begun at first as the glory of the élite, became in time an aspiration and inspiration to the nation at large; and though the populace could not attain the moral height of those loftier souls, yet Yamato Damashii, the Soul of Japan, ultimately came to express the Volksgeist[21] of the Island Realm. If religion is no more than "Morality touched by emotion," as Matthew Arnold[22] defines it, few ethical systems are better entitled to the rank of religion than Bushido. Motoöri[23] has put the mute utterance of the nation into words when he sings:

> Isles of blest Japan!
> Should your Yamato spirit Strangers seek to scan,
> Say—scenting morn's sunlit air, Blows the cherry wild
> and fair!

Yes, the *sakura*[24] has for ages been the favorite of our people and the emblem of our character. Mark particularly the terms of definition which the poet uses, the words the *wild cherry flower scenting the morning sun.*

The Yamato spirit is not a tame, tender plant, but a wild—in

---

[21] German loanword for a unique "national spirit."

[22] Matthew Arnold (1822–88), a British poet. In *Literature and Dogma* (1873) he writes, "Religion, if we follow the intention of human thought and human language in the use of the word, is ethics heightened, enkindled, lit up by feeling; the passage from morality to religion is made when to morality is applied emotion. And the true meaning of religion is thus, not simply *morality*, but *morality touched by emotion."*

[23] Motoori Norinaga (1730–1801), a prominent scholar of Japanese classics.

[24] [*Cerasus pseudo-cerasus*, Lindley.] A species of cherry tree. John Lindley (1799–1865) was an English botanist.

the sense of natural—growth; it is indigenous to the soil; its acci-
dental qualities it may share with the flowers of other lands, but in
its essence it remains the original, spontaneous outgrowth of our
clime. But its nativity is not its sole claim to our affection. The refinement and grace of its beauty appeal to our aesthetic sense as no
other flower can. We cannot share the admiration of the Europeans
for their roses, which lack the simplicity of our flower. Then, too,
the thorns that are hidden beneath the sweetness of the rose, the
tenacity with which she clings to life, as though loath or afraid to
die rather than drop untimely, preferring to rot on her stem; her
showy colors and heavy odors—all these are traits so unlike our
flower, which carries no dagger or poison under its beauty, which
is ever ready to depart life at the call of nature, whose colors are
never gorgeous, and whose light fragrance never palls. Beauty of
color and of form is limited in its showing; it is a fixed quality of
existence, whereas fragrance is volatile, ethereal[25] as the breathing
of life. So in all religious ceremonies frankincense and myrrh[26] play
a prominent part. There is something spiritual in redolence. When
the delicious perfume of the sakura quickens the morning air, as
the sun in its course rises to illumine first the isles of the Far East,
few sensations are more serenely exhilarating than to inhale, as it
were, the very breath of beauteous day.

When the Creator Himself is pictured as making new resolutions in His heart upon smelling a sweet savor (Gen. viii. 21), is it
any wonder that the sweet-smelling season of the cherry blossom
should call forth the whole nation from their little habitations?
Blame them not, if for a time their limbs forget their toil and moil
and their hearts their pangs and sorrows. Their brief pleasure
ended, they return to their daily task with new strength and new
resolutions. Thus in ways more than one is the sakura the flower

---

[25] Heavenly.
[26] A fragrant gum resin used as incense.

of the nation.

Is, then, this flower, so sweet and evanescent, blown whither-soever the wind listeth, and, shedding a puff of perfume, ready to vanish forever, is this flower the type of the Yamato spirit? Is the soul of Japan so frailly mortal?

CHAPTER XVI

Is Bushido Still Alive?

H as Western civilization, in its march through our land, already wiped out every trace of its ancient discipline? It was
a sad thing if a nation's soul could die so fast.

That was a poor soul that could succumb so easily to extraneous influences.

The aggregate of psychological elements which constitute a
national character is as tenacious as the "irreducible elements of
species, of the fins of the fish, of the beak of the bird, of the tooth
of the carnivorous animal." In his recent book, full of shallow as-
severations[1] and brilliant generalizations, M. LeBon[2] says: "The
discoveries due to the intelligence are the common patrimony[3] of
humanity; qualities or defects of character constitute the exclusive
patrimony of each people: they are the firm rock which the waters
must wash day by day for centuries, before they can wear away even
its external asperities." These are strong words and would be highly
worth pondering over, provided there were qualities and defects of
character which *constitute the exclusive patrimony* of each people.
Schematizing theories of this sort had been advanced long before
LeBon began to write his book, and they were exploded long ago by

---

[1] Claims.

[2] [*The Psychology of Peoples*, p. 33.] Gustave LeBon (1841–1931) was a French
social psychologist whose *Les Lois psychologiques de l'évolution des peuples was*
published in 1894.

[3] Ancestry.

Theodor Waitz and Hugh Murray.[4] In studying the various virtues instilled by Bushido, we have drawn upon European sources for comparison and illustrations, and we have seen that no one quality of character was its *exclusive* patrimony. It is true the aggregate of moral qualities presents a quite unique aspect. It is this aggregate which Emerson names a "compound result into which every great force enters as an ingredient."[5] But, instead of making it, as LeBon does, an exclusive patrimony of a race or people, the Concord philosopher calls it "an element which unites the most forcible persons of every country; makes them intelligible and agreeable to each other; and is somewhat so precise that it is at once felt if an individual lack the Masonic sign."[6]

The character, which Bushido stamped on our nation and on the samurai in particular, cannot be said to form "an irreducible element of species," but nevertheless as to the vitality which it retains there is no doubt. Were Bushido a mere physical force, the momentum it has gained in the last seven hundred years could not stop so abruptly. Were it transmitted only by heredity, its influence must be immensely widespread. Just think, as M. Cheysson,[7] a French economist, has calculated, that, supposing there be three generations in a century, "each of us would have in his veins the blood of at least twenty millions of the people living in the year 1000 A.D." The merest peasant that grubs the soil, "bowed by the weight of

---

[4] Theodor Waitz (1821–64), a German psychologist and anthropologist and the author of the six-volume *The Anthropology of Primitive Peoples* (1863). Hugh Murray (1779–1846) was a Scottish geographer who authored many books, including *Historical and Moral: Respecting the Character of Nations, and the Progress of Society* (1808), and *Encyclopaedia of Geography* (1834).

[5] Ralph Waldo Emerson (1803–82), an American essayist. Nitobe cites the "Manners" from Emerson's *Essays: Second Series* (1844).

[6] Secret Freemason handshakes and greetings.

[7] Jean Jacques Emile Cheysson (1836–1910), a French engineer and economist who played an important role in the institutionalization of statistics.

centuries,"[8] has in his veins the blood of ages and is thus brother to us as much as "to the ox."

An unconscious and irresistible power, Bushido has been moving the nation and individuals. It was an honest confession of the race when Yoshida Shôin,[9] one of the most brilliant pioneers of Modern Japan, wrote on the eve of his execution the following stanza:

> Full well I knew this course must end in death;
> It was Yamato spirit urged me on
> To dare whate'er betide.

Unformulated, Bushido was and still is the animating spirit, the motor force of our country.

Mr. Ransome[10] says that "there are three distinct Japans in existence side by side today—the old, which has not wholly died out; the new, hardly yet born except in spirit; and the transition, passing now through its most critical throes." While this is very true in most respects, and particularly as regards tangible and concrete institutions, the statement, as applied to fundamental ethical notions, requires some modification; for Bushido, the maker and product of Old Japan, is still the guiding principle of the transition and will prove the formative force of the new era.

The great statesmen, who steered the ship of our state through the hurricane of the Restoration and the whirlpool of national rejuvenation, were men who knew no other moral teaching than the

---

[8] Nitobe is quoting from Edwin Markham's (1852–1940) poem "The Man with the Hoe" (1898).

[9] Yoshida Shōin (1830–59), an activist samurai from the Chōshū domain who advocated adopting Western technology in order to mitigate Western incursion. He was eventually executed by the shogunate for sedition, but his teachings had a profound influence on a generation of future Japanese leaders.

[10] James Stafford Ransome (1860–1931). Nitobe quotes from *Japan in Transition: A Comparative Study of the Progress, Policy, and Methods of the Japanese Since Their War with China* (1899).

Precepts of Knighthood. Some writers[11] have lately tried to prove that the Christian missionaries contributed an appreciable quota to the making of New Japan. I would fain render honor to whom honor is due; but this honor can as yet hardly be accorded to the good missionaries. More fitting it will be to their profession to stick to the scriptural injunction of preferring one another in honor, than to advance a claim in which they have no proofs to back them. For myself, I believe that Christian missionaries are doing great things for Japan—in the domain of education, and especially of moral education—only, the mysterious though not the less certain working of the Spirit is still hidden in divine secrecy. Whatever they do is still of indirect effect. No, as yet Christian missions have effected but little visible in molding the character of New Japan. No, it was Bushido, pure and simple, that urged us on for weal or woe. Open the biographies of the makers of Modern Japan—of Sakuma, of Saigo, of Okubo, of Kido,[12] not to mention the reminiscences of living men such as Ito, Okuma, Itagaki, etc.—and you will find that it was under the impetus of samuraihood that they thought and wrought. When Mr. Henry Norman declared, after his study and observation of the Far East that the only respect in which Japan differed from other oriental despotisms lay in "the ruling influence among her people of the strictest, loftiest, and the most punctilious codes of honor that man has ever devised," he touched the mainspring which has made New Japan what she is, and which will make

---

11 [Speer, *Missions and Politics in Asia*, Lecture IV, pp. 189–92; Dennis, *Christian Missions and Social Progress*, vol. i, p. 32, vol. ii, p. 70, etc.] Robert E. Speer (1867–1947) was an American missionary and the author of *Missions and Politics in Asia* (1898). James S. Dennis (1842–1914) was an American missionary to Syria and the author of *Christian Missions and Social Progress; A Sociological Study of Foreign Missions* (1897).

12 All leaders of modern Japan during the Meiji period. Sakuma Shōzan (1811–64), Saigō Takamori (1827–77), Ōkubo Toshimichi (1830–78), Kido Takayoshi (1833–77), Itō Hirobumi (1841–1909), Ōkuma Shigenobu (1838–1922) and Itagaki Taisuke (1837–1919).

her what she is destined to be.[13]

The transformation of Japan is a fact patent to the whole world. Into a work of such magnitude various motives naturally entered; but if one were to name the principal, one would not hesitate to name Bushido.

When we opened the whole country to foreign trade, when we introduced the latest improvements in every department of life, when we began to study Western politics and sciences, our guiding motive was not the development of our physical resources and the increase of wealth; much less was it a blind imitation of Western customs.

A close observer of oriental institutions and peoples has written:

> We are told every day how Europe has influenced Japan, and forget that the change in those islands was entirely self-generated, that Europeans did not teach Japan, but that Japan of herself chose to learn from Europe methods of organization, civil and military, which have so far proved successful. She imported European mechanical science, as the Turks years before imported European artillery. That is not exactly influence," continues Mr. Townsend, "unless, indeed, England is influenced by purchasing tea in China. Where is the European apostle," asks our author, "or philosopher or statesman or agitator, who has remade Japan?[14]

Mr. Townsend has well perceived that the spring of action which brought about the changes in Japan lay entirely within our own selves; and if he had only probed into our psychology, his keen

---

[13] [*The Far East*, p. 375.]

[14] [Meredith Townsend, *Asia and Europe*, p. 28.] Meredith Townsend (1831–1911) was an English journalist. Nitobe quotes from his *Asia and Europe* (1901).

powers of observation would easily have convinced him that this spring was no other than Bushido. The sense of honor which cannot bear being looked down upon as an inferior power—that was the strongest of motives. Pecuniary or industrial considerations were awakened later in the process of transformation.

The influence of Bushido is still so palpable that he who runs may read. A glimpse into Japanese life will make it manifest. Read Hearn, the most eloquent and truthful interpreter of the Japanese mind, and you see the working of that mind to be an example of the working of Bushido. The universal politeness of the people, which is the legacy of knightly ways, is too well known to be repeated anew. The physical endurance, fortitude, and bravery that "the little Jap" possesses, were sufficiently proved in the Sino-Japanese war.[15] "Is there any nation more loyal and patriotic?" is a question asked by many; and for the proud answer, "There is not," we must thank the Precepts of Knighthood.

On the other hand, it is fair to recognize that for the very faults and defects of our character, Bushido is largely responsible. Our lack of abstruse philosophy—while some of our young men have already gained international reputation in scientific researches, not one has achieved anything in philosophical lines—is traceable to the neglect of metaphysical training under Bushido's regimen of education. Our sense of honor is responsible for our exaggerated sensitiveness and touchiness; and if there is the conceit in us with which some foreigners charge us, that, too, is a pathological outcome of honor.

---

[15] [Among other works on the subject, read Eastlake and Yamada on *Heroic Japan* and *Doisy* on *The New Far East*.] F. Warrington Eastlake (1858–1905) and Yamada Yoshiaki (dates unknown) co-wrote *Heroic Japan: A History of the War between China and Japan* (1897). Yamada was possible the Methodist minister Yamada Toranosuke (1861–1928).

Arthur Doisy (1856–1923) was the founder of the Japan Society of London and the author of *The New Far East* (1899).

Have you seen in your tour of Japan many a young man with unkempt hair, dressed in shabbiest garb, carrying in his hand a large cane or a book, stalking about the streets with an air of utter indifference to mundane things? He is the *shoséi* (student), to whom the earth is too small and the heavens are not high enough. He has his own theories of the universe and of life. He dwells in castles of air and feeds on ethereal words of wisdom. In his eyes beams the fire of ambition; his mind is athirst for knowledge. Penury is only a stimulus to drive him onward; worldly goods are in his sight shackles to his character. He is the repository of loyalty and patriotism. He is the self-imposed guardian of national honor. With all his virtues and his faults, he is the last fragment of Bushido.

Deep-rooted and powerful as is still the effect of Bushido, I have said that it is an unconscious and mute influence. The heart of the people responds, without knowing a reason why, to any appeal made to what it has inherited, and hence the same moral idea expressed in a newly translated term and in an old Bushido term, has a vastly different degree of efficacy. A backsliding Christian, whom no pastoral persuasion could help from downward tendency, was reverted from his course by an appeal made to his loyalty, the fidelity he once swore to his Master. The word "Loyalty" revived all the noble sentiments that were permitted to grow lukewarm. A party of unruly youths engaged in a long-continued "students' strike"[16] in a college, on account of their dissatisfaction with a certain teacher, disbanded at two simple questions put by the Director—"Is your professor a worthy character? If so, you ought to respect him and keep him in the school. Is he weak? If so, it is not manly to push a falling man." The scientific incapacity of the professor, which was the beginning of the trouble, dwindled into insignificance in com-

[16] It is not certain what Nitobe is referring to in these accounts, but it is possibly something to do with dissent in his student days at the Sapporo Agricultural College.

parison with the moral issues hinted at. By arousing the sentiments nurtured by Bushido, moral renovation of great magnitude can be accomplished.

One cause of the failure of mission work is that most of the missionaries are entirely ignorant of our history—"What do we care for heathen records?" some say—and consequently estrange their religion from the habits of thought we and our forefathers have been accustomed to for centuries past. Mocking a nation's history?—as though the career of any people—even of the lowest African savages possessing no record—were not a page in the general history of mankind, written by the hand of God Himself. The very lost races are a palimpsest[17] to be deciphered by a seeing eye. To a philosophic and pious mind the races themselves are marks of Divine chirography clearly traced in black and white as on their skin; and if this simile holds good, the yellow race forms a precious page inscribed in hieroglyphics of gold! Ignoring the past career of a people, missionaries claim that Christianity is a new religion, whereas, to my mind, it is an "old, old story," which, if presented in intelligible words—that is to say, if expressed in the vocabulary familiar in the moral development of a people, will find easy lodgment in their hearts, irrespective of race or nationality. Christianity in its American or English form—with more of Anglo-Saxon freaks and fancies than grace and purity of its Founder—is a poor scion to graft on Bushido stock. Should the propagator of the new faith uproot the entire stock, root, and branches, and plant the seeds of the Gospel on the ravaged soil? Such a heroic process may be possible—in Hawaii, where, it is alleged, the Church militant had complete success in amassing spoils of wealth itself, and in annihilating the aboriginal race; such a process is most decidedly impossible in Japan—nay, it is a process which Jesus Himself would never have adopted in founding His kingdom on earth.

---

[17] A manuscript page from a scroll or a book.

It behooves us to take more to heart the following words of a saintly man, devout Christian, and profound scholar:

> Men have divided the world into heathen and Christian, without considering how much good may have been hidden in the one or how much evil may have been mingled with the other. They have compared the best part of themselves with the worst of their neighbors, the ideal of Christianity with the corruption of Greece or of the East. They have not aimed at impartiality, but have been contented to accumulate all that could be said in praise of their own, and in dispraise of other forms of religion.[18]

But, whatever may be the error committed by individuals, there is little doubt that the fundamental principle of the religion they profess is a power which we must take into account in reckoning the future of Bushido, whose days seem to be already numbered. Ominous signs are in the air that betoken its future. Not only signs, but redoubtable forces are at work to threaten it.

---

[18] [Jowett, *Sermons on Faith and Doctrine*, ii.] Benjamin Jowett (1817–93) was a British classical scholar and theologian whose *Sermons on Faith and Doctrine* was published posthumously in 1901.

lectual parvenu[3] of the type of Bentham and Mill.[4] Moral theories of a comfortable kind, flattering to the Chauvinistic tendencies of the time, and therefore thought well adapted to the need of this day, have been invented and propounded; but as yet we hear only their shrill voices echoing through the columns of yellow journalism.[5]

Principalities and powers are arrayed against the Precepts of Knighthood. Already, as Veblen says, "the decay of the ceremonial code—or, as it is otherwise called, the vulgarization of life—among the industrial classes proper, has become one of the chief enormities of latter-day civilization in the eyes of all persons of delicate sensibilities."[6] The irresistible tide of triumphant democracy, which can tolerate no form or shape of trust—and Bushido was a trust organized by those who monopolized reserve capital of intellect and culture, fixing the grades and value of moral qualities—is alone powerful enough to engulf the remnant of Bushido. The present societary forces are antagonistic to petty class spirit, and chivalry is, as Freeman[7] severely criticizes, a class spirit. Modern society, if it pretends to any unity, cannot admit "purely personal obligations devised in the interests of an exclusive class."[8] Add to this the progress of popular instruction, of industrial arts and habits, of wealth and city life then we can easily see that neither the keenest cuts of

---

[3] A person who has recently acquired importance but has not yet developed the appropriate manners.

[4] English philosophers Jeremy Bentham (1748–1832) and John Stewart Mill (1806–73) who advocated the doctrine of utilitarianism in which working for the greater good brings happiness and is therefore the correct action.

[5] A style of [tabloid] newspaper reporting that emphasized sensationalism over facts.

[6] Thorstein Bunde Veblen (1857–1929), an American economist who wrote *The Theory of the Leisure Class: An Economic Study of Institutions* (1899).

[7] Edward Augustus Freeman (1823–92), an English historian at the University of Oxford who published *The History of the Norman Conquest of England* between 1867and 1876.

[8] [*Norman Conquest*, vol. v, p. 482.]

The Future of Bushido

F ew historical comparisons can be more judiciously made than between the Chivalry of Europe and the Bushido of Japan, and, if history repeats itself, it certainly will do with the fate of the latter what it did with that of the former. The particular and local causes for the decay of chivalry which St. Palaye[1] gives, have, of course, little application to Japanese conditions; but the larger and more general causes that helped to undermine knighthood and chivalry in and after the Middle Ages are as surely working for the decline of Bushido.

One remarkable difference between the experience of Europe and of Japan is, that whereas in Europe, when chivalry was weaned from feudalism and was adopted by the Church, it obtained a fresh lease of life, in Japan no religion was large enough to nourish it; hence, when the mother institution, feudalism, was gone, Bushido, left an orphan, had to shift for itself. The present elaborate military organization might take it under its patronage, but we know that modern warfare can afford little room for its continuous growth. Shintoism, which fostered it in its infancy, is itself superannuated.[2] The hoary sages of ancient China are being supplanted by the intel-

---

[1] Jean-Baptiste de La Curne de Sainte-Palaye (1697–1781), a French historian who wrote on the origins of chivalry in *Mémoires sur l'ancienne chevalerie* (Memoirs of Ancient Chivalry, 1759).

[2] Old-fashioned.

samurai sword nor the sharpest shafts shot from Bushido's boldest bows can aught avail. The state built upon the rock of Honor and fortified by the same—shall we call it the *Ehrenstaat*,[9] or, after the manner of Carlyle, the Heroarchy?[10]—is fast falling into the hands of quibbling lawyers and gibbering politicians armed with logic-chopping engines of war. The words which a great thinker used in speaking of Theresa and Antigone[11] may aptly be repeated of the samurai, that "the medium in which their ardent deeds took shape is forever gone."[12]

Alas for knightly virtues! Alas for samurai pride! Morality, ushered into the world with the sound of bugles and drums, is destined to fade away as "the captains and the kings depart."[13]

If history can teach us anything, the state built on martial virtues—be it a city like Sparta or an Empire like Rome—can never make on earth a "continuing city."[14] Universal and natural as is the fighting instinct in man, fruitful as it has proved to be of noble sentiments and manly virtues, it does not comprehend the whole man. Beneath the instinct to fight there lurks a diviner instinct—to love. We have seen that Shintoism, Mencius, and Wan Yang Ming, have all clearly taught it; but Bushido and all other militant types of ethics, engrossed doubtless with questions of immediate practical need, too often forgot duly to emphasize this fact. Life has grown

---

[9] A German word Nitobe made meaning "Honor State."

[10] A government of heroes. The idea of Heroarchy, where society is premised on hero worship, is expounded on in Carlyle's *On Heroes, Hero-Worship and the Heroic in History* (1840).

[11] Saint Teresa of Ávila (1515–82). Antigone is a mythical character in Sophocles' play (441 BC) who hangs herself after being punished by the king for daring to bury her disgraced brother.

[12] Quoted from English novelist George Eliot's (pseudonym for Mary Ann Evans, 1819–80) *Middlemarch* (1871–72).

[13] A reference to Rudyard Kipling's (1865–1936) poem "Recessional" (1897).

[14] Hebrews 13:14 in which Jesus says, "For here we have no continuing city, but we seek one to come."

larger in these latter times. Callings nobler and broader than a warrior's claim our attention today. With an enlarged view of life, with the growth of democracy, with better knowledge of other peoples and nations, the Confucian idea of benevolence—dare I also add the Buddhist idea of pity?—will expand into the Christian conception of love. Men have become more than subjects, having grown to the estate of citizens; nay, they are more than citizens—being men. Though war clouds hang heavy upon our horizon, we will believe that the wings of the angel of peace can disperse them. The history of the world confirms the prophecy that "the meek shall inherit the earth."[15] A nation that sells its birthright of peace, and backslides from the front rank of industrialism into the file of filibusterism,[16] makes a poor bargain indeed!

When the conditions of society are so changed that they have become not only adverse but hostile to Bushido, it is time for it to prepare for an honorable burial. It is just as difficult to point out when chivalry dies, as to determine the exact time of its inception. Dr. Miller says that chivalry was formally abolished in the year 1559, when Henry II of France was slain in a tournament.[17] With us, the edict formally abolishing feudalism in 1870[18] was the signal to toll the knell of Bushido. The edict, issued five years later, prohibiting the wearing of swords,[19] rang out the old, "the unbought grace of life, the cheap defense of nations, the nurse of manly sentiment and heroic enterprise," and rang in the new age of "sophisters, economists, and calculators."[20]

---

[15] Matthew 5:5.

[16] Engaging in unsanctioned conflict.

[17] George Miller (1764–1848). In *History, Philosophically Illustrated, from the Fall of the Roman Empire, to the French Revolution* (1832), Miller states that chivalry was "abolished" in 1559.

[18] This should be 1871.

[19] *Haitōrei* (Sword Banning Edict) of 1876.

[20] Nitobe quotes from Edmund Burke's (1729–97) *Reflections on the Revolution in France* (1790).

It has been said that Japan won her late war with China by means of Murata guns and Krupp cannon;²¹ it has been said the victory was the work of a modern school-system; but these are less than half-truths. Does ever a piano, be it of the choicest workmanship of Ehrbar or Steinway²² burst forth into the Rhapsodies of Liszt²³ or the Sonatas of Beethoven,²⁴ without a master's hand? Or, if guns win battles, why did not Louis Napoleon²⁵ beat the Prussians with his *Mitrailleuse*, or the Spaniards with their Mausers²⁶ the Filipinos, whose arms were no better than the old-fashioned Remingtons? Needless to repeat what has grown a trite saying—that it is the spirit that quickeneth,²⁷ without which the best of implements profiteth but little. The most improved guns and cannon do not shoot of their own accord; the most modern educational system does not make a coward a hero. No! What won the battles on the Yalu,²⁸ in Korea and Manchuria, were the ghosts of our fathers, guiding our hands and beating in our hearts. They are not dead, those ghosts, the spirits of our warlike ancestors. To those who have eyes to see, they are clearly visible. Scratch a Japanese of the most advanced ideas, and he will show a samurai. The great inheritance of honor, of valor, and of all martial virtues is, as Professor Cramb very fitly expresses it, "but ours on trust, the fief inalienable of the dead and

---

²¹ The Murata Rifle was the first rifle produced in Japan for the modern Japanese military in 1880. The Krupp Works made the first steel cannon in 1847. The company manufactured arms for many countries in the nineteenth century.

²² Well-known piano manufacturers.

²³ Franz Liszt (1811–86), a Hungarian composer and pianist.

²⁴ Ludwig van Beethoven (1770–1827), a German composer.

²⁵ Charles Louis Napoleon Bonaparte (Napoleon III, 1808–73), Emperor of France from 1852 to 1870.

²⁶ The Spanish army used German-made M93 Mausers in the Philippine Revolution of 1896–98.

²⁷ John 6:63. "It is the spirit that quickeneth; the flesh profiteth nothing: the words that I speak unto you, they are spirit, and they are life."

²⁸ The Yalu River (Amnok River) is on the border between North Korea and China.

of the generations to come,"[29] and the summons of the present is
to guard this heritage, nor to bate one jot of the ancient spirit; the
summons of the future will be so to widen its scope as to apply it
in all walks and relations of life.

It has been predicted—and predictions have been corroborated by the events of the last half-century—that the moral system
of Feudal Japan, like its castles and its armories, will crumble into
dust, and new ethics rise phoenix-like to lead New Japan in her
path of progress. Desirable and probable as the fulfillment of such
a prophecy is, we must not forget that a phoenix rises only from
its own ashes, and that it is not a bird of passage, neither does it fly
on pinions[30] borrowed from other birds. "The Kingdom of God is
within you."[31] It does not come rolling down the mountains, however lofty; it does not come sailing across the seas, however broad.
"God has granted," says the Koran,[32] "to every people a prophet in
its own tongue." The seeds of the Kingdom, as vouched for and
apprehended by the Japanese mind, blossomed in Bushido. Now
its days are closing—sad to say, before its full fruition—and we
turn in every direction for other sources of sweetness and light,
of strength and comfort, but among them there is as yet nothing
found to take its place. The profit-and loss philosophy of utilitar-
ians and materialists[33] finds favor among logic-choppers with half
a soul. The only other ethical system which is powerful enough to

---

[29] John Adam Cramb (1862–1913), a Scottish historian and writer. Quoted from
his *Reflections on the Origins and Destiny of Imperial Britain* (1900).

[30] Wings or feathers.

[31] Luke 17:20–21. "And when he was demanded of the Pharisees, when the kingdom of God should come, he answered them and said, The kingdom of God
cometh not with observation: Neither shall they say, Lo here! or, lo there! for,
behold, the kingdom of God is within you."

[32] Quoted from Emerson's *Representative Men: Seven Lectures*.

[33] "Utilitarianism" in which happiness for the greater good of society is the utilitarian result of right action. "Materialism" being the idea that all things can be
rationalized in terms of physical matter and phenomena.

cope with utilitarianism and materialism is Christianity, in comparison with which Bushido, it must be confessed, is like "a dimly burning wick"[34] which the Messiah was proclaimed not to quench, but to fan into a flame. Like His Hebrew precursors, the prophets—notably Isaiah, Jeremiah, Amos, and Habakkuk[35]—Bushido laid particular stress on the moral conduct of rulers and public men and of nations, whereas the ethics of Christ, which deal almost solely with individuals and His personal followers, will find more and more practical application as individualism, in its capacity of a moral factor, grows in potency. The domineering, self-assertive, so-called master-morality of Nietzsche,[36] itself akin in some respects to Bushido, is, if I am not greatly mistaken, a passing phase or temporary reaction against what he terms, by morbid distortion, the humble, self-denying slave-morality of the Nazarene.[37]

Christianity and materialism (including utilitarianism)—or will the future reduce them to still more archaic forms of Hebraism[38] and Hellenism?[39]—will divide the world between them. Lesser systems of morals will ally themselves to either side for their preservation. On which side will Bushido enlist? Having no set dogma or formula to defend, it can afford to disappear as an entity; like the cherry blossom, it is willing to die at the first gust of the morning breeze. But a total extinction will never be its lot. Who can say that stoicism is dead? It is dead as a system; but it is alive as a virtue: its energy and vitality are still felt through many channels of life—in the philosophy of Western nations, in the jurisprudence of all the

---

[34] Isaiah 42:3.

[35] Isaiah was an eighth-century BC prophet of Judah. Jeremiah, Amos and Habukkuk were Hebrew prophets active from the sixth to eighth centuries BC.

[36] Friedrich Wilhelm Nietzsche (1844–1900), a German philosopher who criticized notions of Christian morality.

[37] Jesus of Nazareth.

[38] A characteristic feature of Hebrew occurring in another language.

[39] Imitation or adoption of ancient Greek language, thought, customs, art, etc.

civilized world. Nay, wherever man struggles to raise himself above himself, wherever his spirit masters his flesh by his own exertions, there we see the immortal discipline of Zeno at work.[40]

Bushido as an independent code of ethics may vanish, but its power will not perish from the earth; its schools of martial prowess or civic honor may be demolished, but its light and its glory will long survive their ruins. Like its symbolic flower, after it is blown to the four winds, it will still bless mankind with the perfume with which it will enrich life. Ages after, when its customaries will have been buried and its very name forgotten, its odors will come floating in the air as from a far-off, unseen hill, "the wayside gaze beyond"—then in the beautiful language of the Quaker poet,

> The traveler owns the grateful sense
> Of sweetness near, he knows not whence,
> And, pausing, takes with forehead bare
> The benediction of the air.[41]

---

[40] Zeno of Citium (c. 335–c. 263 BC), a Greek philosopher credited with founding Stoicism.

[41] Nitobe quotes from John Greenleaf Whittier's (1807–92) poem "Snow-Bound" (1865).

Index

In pronouncing Japanese names, use the Continental European sounds of vowels, and consonants according to the usual values in English, giving the hard sound of *g*; *e* at the end of a syllable, as in Nitobe, Shigemori, Tametomo, etc., is as *e* in *prey*. In some names, as in Iyéyasu˘ (final *u* being short), we have used accents.

of, 64-71; and the state, 27, 61, 63, 130; teaching of, 118–119, 86; view of knowledge, 11

C

Caesar, Julius, 61
Calligraphy, 120
Camillus, 80
Carlyle, Thomas, 106, 179
Cha-no-yu (Tea ceremony), 94–95
Chastity, 151
Cherry blossom, 164
Cheysson, Jean Jacques Emile, 169
Chikamatsu, 162
China, war with, 126, 173
Chivalry, 58–59, 63, 177; death of, 180; in Japan, 57–59; and loyalty, 110; and money, 120. *See also* Bushido and Bushido
Chi (wisdom), 119
Christ, 15–16, 55, 107. *See also* Christianity
Christianity, 63, 90, 155, 175, 183; medieval church, 67; missionaries in Japan, 171, 175; revivals in Japan, 127; and war, 63
Christians, 99, 117, 133. *See also* Christianity

Commerce, 100–103; status of, 101
Complaisance, 90
Confucius: *Analects*, 68, 76; *Doctrine of the Mean*, 98; five moral relations of, 67; *Great Learning*, 82; on revenge, 141; sayings of, 76, 81, 82, 92, 122
Conscience, definition of, 69
Courage, 41, 76–80, 119; moral or physical, 77; stories of children's, 77
Courtesy. *See* Politeness
Cramb, Professor, 181
Crito, 115

D

Dante, 138
Dean, Professor, 91
Declaration of Independence, 157
Democritus, 128–129
Dennis, James S., 171n11
Descartes, René, 132
Despotism: Oriental, 82; and paternal government, 83–84
Dhyâna, 64
Dill, Samuel, 101
Doisy, Arthur, 173n15
Doctrine of the Mean (Confucius), 98
Don Quixote, 121